Clusters of Competitiveness

DIRECTIONS IN DEVELOPMENT
Private Sector Development

Clusters of Competitiveness

Raj Nallari and Breda Griffith

THE WORLD BANK
Washington, D.C.

Library of Congress Cataloging-in-Publication Data

Nallari, Raj, 1955–
Clusters of competitiveness / Raj Nallari, Breda Griffith.
      pages cm. — (Directions in development)
   Includes bibliographical references.
ISBN 978-1-4648-0049-8 (alk. paper) — ISBN 978-1-4648-0050-4 (ebk.)
   1. Competition. 2. Economic development. I. Griffith, Breda. II. World Bank. III. Title.
   HB238.N35 2013
   338.6'048—dc23   2013022140

Contents

Tables

Preface

Competition, competitiveness, innovation, and growth are inherently linked and thus provide a compelling basis for policy analysis and recommendations. A favorable macroeconomy featuring sound policies and stable institutions is necessary for prosperity. Prosperity also depends upon competitiveness, which arises from the microeconomic foundations of a society. How companies operate and the quality of the business environment in which they compete are some of the microeconomic issues underlying competitiveness. The modern, knowledge-driven globalized economy is a product of innovation and competitiveness. Understanding the factors affecting the innovation decisions of firms and industries is critical for the design and ultimate success of policy.

Competitiveness is a broad subject with applications at the level of the firm, industry, region, nation, and global economy. Each one of these aspects has a rich literature drawn on by academics and policy makers over a long period. This book seeks to present a broad overview of the main ideas underlying competitiveness and its applications, highlighting and discussing in greater depth the topics that are of relevance currently. Specifically, the book draws out the experiences of and lessons for developing economies and examines in detail the role for policy.

Chapter 1 addresses competition and competition policy. Competition is good for growth and is the hallmark of the market economy. For example, competition in product markets is an important determinant of economic growth. Competition can lead to gains in productivity, or more technically to multifactor productivity, that is, combined productivity gains in labor and capital. The extent of regulation in product markets is an indicator of how supportive an economy is of competition. In general, tighter regulation is negatively associated with economic growth, while improved governance lessens the negative effects of regulation. As developing economies proceed with market-oriented reform, competition policy is critical in ensuring favorable efficiency and welfare benefits to society at large.

Chapter 2 examines competitiveness by analyzing its many different indicators. Classifying competitiveness is difficult, although some broad classifications provide a framework in which to discuss this aspect of the economy. Competitiveness may be examined across narrow and broad measures, macro and micro indicators, short-term and long-term indicators, and price and nonprice measures. A competitive economy is a successful economy, and economists have long grappled with the reasons why some economies grow or are more successful than others. The chapter begins by looking at what it means to be competitive in a national and international sense and then examines some narrow and broad measures of competitiveness before considering the macroeconomic and microeconomic factors affecting the indicators of competitiveness. The chapter concludes with an examination of the international surveys of competitiveness and their complementarity in presenting indexes of national competitiveness.

Chapter 3 looks further at indexes of national competitiveness that describe international competitive performance. From these indexes, top-ranking countries for competitiveness in 2012 are identified. The chapter addresses price and nonprice measures of competitiveness. It examines three surveys related to nonprice measures of competitiveness: those of the Institute for Management Development, the World Economic Forum, and the World Bank. The respective publications are the World Competitiveness Scoreboard, the Global Competitiveness Index, and the Ease of Doing Business Index. The real effective exchange rate (REER) based on unit labor costs and on inflation (as indicated by the consumer price index) is charted for a set of wealthy, highly productive countries for competitiveness based on nonprice measures.

Chapter 4 addresses innovation, an increasingly important aspect of competitiveness. Innovation is a leading characteristic of the modern knowledge-driven economy. It also plays a crucial role in developing economies wishing to catch up in economic growth and development to developed countries. It is the basis of sustainable economic growth and is critical for addressing the global challenges confronting the world today. Innovation is a major objective of national policy. The chapter highlights the role played by innovation in economic growth and competitiveness before moving to an examination of the elements for an innovation policy that contributes to the pursuit of competitiveness.

Chapter 5 discusses competitiveness and clusters. Cluster development has been embraced by policy makers as a way of stimulating an area's economic development and growth. Clusters are systems of interconnectedness between private and public sector entities. They are usually made up of a group of companies, suppliers, service providers, and associated institutions in a particular field or industry. Policy has sought to encourage cluster development through government involvement in cluster-based competitiveness projects. Other policies in science and technology, regional policy, and industrial policy also have implications for cluster development. The chapter looks at the background of cluster development and competitiveness and then addresses cluster initiatives and cluster-based competitiveness projects. It also examines public policy in this area.

About the Authors

Raj Nallari is the practice manager for the growth and competitiveness practice at the World Bank Institute (WBI). He has worked at the World Bank for more than 20 years in various departments. Previously he worked at the International Monetary Fund. Raj has published on various topics, including growth adjustment systems, the labor market and gender, and macroeconomics. He has also edited several volumes of *Development Outreach*. He holds a PhD in economics from the University of Texas at Austin.

Breda Griffith has worked as a consultant with the WBI since 2005 in the areas of growth, poverty, gender, development, and labor markets. She has publications in refereed journals on development and language maintenance, entrepreneurship, and small business. Breda has also coauthored books on economic growth, poverty, gender and macroeconomic policy, new directions in development, labor markets in developing countries, and geography of growth. She has developed and facilitated e-learning courses in these areas. She holds a PhD in economics from Trinity College Dublin, Ireland, and an MA in economics from the National University of Ireland.

Abbreviations

ASEAN	Association of Southeast Asian Nations
BMA	Bayesian model averaging
CAF	Competition Assessment Framework
CDM	Clean Development Mechanism
CEEP	Centre for Public Enterprises with Public Participation
CI	cluster initiative
CPI	consumer price index
ECB	European Central Bank
FDI	foreign direct investment
GCI	Global Competitiveness Index
GDP	gross domestic product
GNI	gross national income
HCIs	harmonized competitiveness indicators
ICT	information and communication technology
IFS	International Financial Statistics
IMD	International Institute for Management Development
IMF	International Monetary Fund
ISIC	International Standard Industrial Classification
IT	information technology
M&A	mergers and acquisitions
MFP	multifactor productivity
NIEs	newly industrialized economies
OECD	Organisation for Economic Co-operation and Development
PMR	product market regulation
R&D	research and development
REER	real effective exchange rate
SAR	special administrative region
SIC	standard industrial classification
SIPIs	social infrastructure and political institutions

SME	small and medium enterprise
SWOT	strengths, weaknesses, opportunities, and threats
TCD	trade competitiveness diagnostic
TFP	total factor productivity
WCY	*World Competitiveness Yearbook*
WEF	World Economic Forum
WTO	World Trade Organization

CHAPTER 1

Competition, Competition Policy, and Growth

Competition is good for growth and is a prime characteristic of the market economy. For example, competition in product markets is an important determinant of economic growth. Competition can lead to one-time (static) and ongoing (dynamic) gains in productivity or more technically to multifactor productivity, that is, combined productivity gains in labor and capital. Examples of one-off gains are better resource allocation and less slack in the use of inputs. Dynamic gains are associated with greater tendencies to innovate and the distribution of innovation.

The extent of regulation in product markets is an indicator of how supportive an economy is of competition. In general, tighter regulation is negatively associated with economic growth, while improved governance lessens the negative effects of regulation. Thus, economic growth in higher-income countries is positively related to deregulation, but at lower-income levels, we need to look more closely at the competition/regulation trade-off. The degree of competition is important.

Competition stimulates economic growth within the overall macroeconomy. As developing economies proceed with market-oriented reform, competition policy is critical in ensuring favorable efficiency and welfare benefits to society at large. Competition policy has an important role to play in promoting growth. Furthermore, competition policy affects competitiveness, domestically and internationally.

The following sections examine the relationship between competition and growth and focus on the policy aspects of this relationship.

Competition and Growth

Competition in economics is defined as free entry and exit of firms in any market. The theoretical literature on competition and economic growth is prolific, with many facets, yet devoid of any firm conclusion (Yun 2004). Hence, the empirical studies have been useful in shedding light on the relationship between competition and growth.

One area of study has been the impact of product market competition on productivity gains, with key studies in this area confirming a positive relationship between competition and productivity growth.[1] Product market competition is but one factor among many that affect aggregate performance indicators, such as employment and productivity. Nevertheless, work by the Organisation for Economic Co-operation and Development (OECD 2002, 155) "has identified an empirical connection between strong competition in markets for goods and services and better productivity and employment outcomes." Moreover, differences in competitive pressures play an important part in explaining the differences in productivity across countries.

Competition affects per capita growth through its effect on productivity. As noted, increases in productivity arise from both static and dynamic efficiency gains. Regulatory reform that stimulates managerial effort is an example of a static efficiency gain.[2] Medium- and long-term gains in productivity—dynamic efficiency gains—arise from investments in research and development (R&D), product and process innovation, and the associated buildup of human capital (Høj et al. 2007). There is an established empirical relationship between innovation and growth, with some dispute on the effects of competition on innovation.[3] The long-run effects of competition are likely to be positive on aggregate labor productivity growth. Lower price-cost margins arising from increased competition lead to job creation and upward pressure on average real wages. Further, lower product-market rents imply lower wage premium in some sectors, thus reducing labor costs and encouraging job creation. An increase of 1.5–2.5 percent in the employment rate may be observed where in-depth reforms have been adopted (Høj et al. 2007). On this point, see Høj et al. (2007), who refer to the work of Alesina et al. (2005), Nicoletti and Scarpetta (2003), and Conway et al. (2006).[4]

Høj et al. (2007) examine the data on price-cost margins (markups) for 17 countries in the OECD as a measure of competition. Figure 1.1 shows the results for the four different groups of manufacturing industries identified in table 1.1. These industries were identified along two dimensions[5]—the level of exogenous sunk costs (which identifies whether industries are fragmented or segmented) and the level of endogenous sunk costs (low or high R&D and advertising expenditures) and the markups for nonmanufacturing industries.

The cross-country mean of markups for the four manufacturing industries, shown in figure 1.1, are not statistically different from one another. Greater variation is evident in the nonmanufacturing industry markups—average markups are estimated to be below 20 percent in the United Kingdom, Sweden, and the United States; higher for most European countries; and highest for the Republic of Korea (32 percent) and Italy (38 percent) (Høj 2007). Table 1.1 sheds light on the underlying data.

Høj et al. (2007) attribute the greater variability in nonmanufacturing industries to a relative absence of competitive pressures in services compared to

Figure 1.1　Markups in Manufacturing and Nonmanufacturing

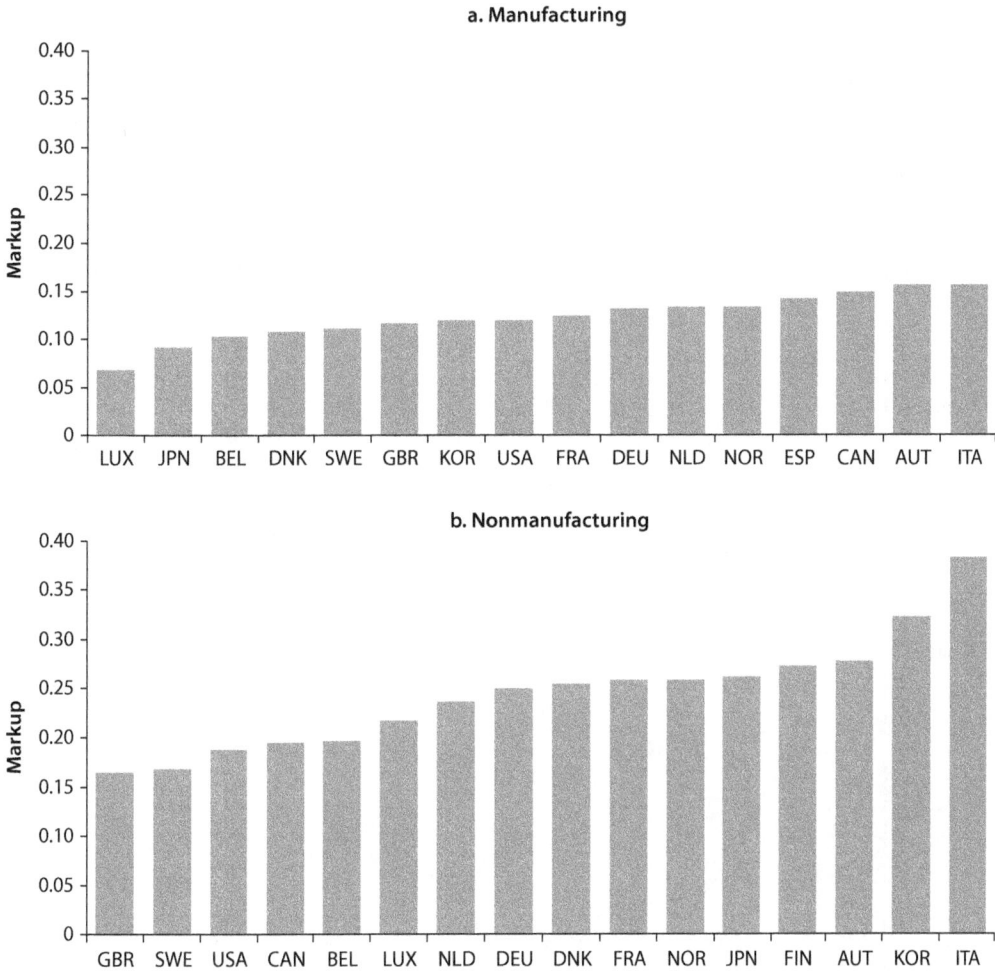

a. Manufacturing

b. Nonmanufacturing

Source: Høj et al. 2007, 53.

Note: GBR = Great Britain; SWE = Sweden; USA = United States; CAN = Canada; BEL = Belgium; LUX = Luxembourg; NLD = Netherlands; DEU = Germany; DNK = Denmark; FRA = France; NOR = Norway; JPN = Japan; FIN = Finland; AUT = Australia; KOR = Korea, Rep.; ITA = Italy; ESP = Spain. Markups are calculated for individual 2-digit International Standard Industrial Classification (ISIC) sectors and aggregated over all sectors using country-specific final sales as weights.

manufacturing and the diversity of competition policies being pursued in the sample countries.

Product Market Regulation and Economic Performance

There is a fairly extensive empirical literature on the macroeconomic effects of regulatory reform in the labor and financial markets, while "the area that has been comparatively under-researched is the effect of product market regulation (PMR) on macroeconomic outcomes, with the exception of the effect of barriers to trade" (Schiantarelli 2008). Nicoletti and Scarpetta (2005) concur and note

Table 1.1 Markups Estimates by Industry

	Austria	Belgium	Canada	Germany	Denmark	Spain	Finland	France	United Kingdom	Italy	Japan	Korea, Rep.	Luxembourg	Netherlands	Norway	Sweden	United States
All manufacturing	0.15	0.10	0.15	0.13	0.11	0.14	0.18	0.12	0.11	0.15	0.09	0.12	0.07	0.13	0.13	0.11	0.12
Fragmented low-R&D industries:	0.16	0.11	0.19	0.14	0.13	0.16	0.21	0.12	0.12	0.18	0.08	0.12	0.04	0.16	0.13	0.10	0.13
Textiles, wearing apparel, leather	0.13	0.05	0.13	0.14	0.12	0.13	0.14	0.09	0.10	0.16	0.06	0.12	—	0.14	0.12	—	0.09
Wood and wood products	0.10	0.12	0.25	0.14	0.18	0.16	0.19	0.05	0.16	0.22	0.05	0.13	-0.03	0.08	0.11	—	0.19
Pulp, paper, printing, and publishing	0.19	0.14	0.20	0.19	0.10	0.18	0.23	0.13	0.12	0.18	0.10	0.11	0.10	0.20	0.14	—	0.13
Other nonmetallic mineral products	0.24	0.17	0.22	0.19	0.17	0.19	0.24	0.16	0.16	0.22	0.15	0.18	0.03	0.20	0.14	0.05	0.17
Fabricated metal products	0.13	—	0.13	0.07	—	—	0.16	—	—	0.19	0.01	0.10	0.03	0.11	0.13	0.12	0.12
Segmented low-R&D industries:	0.17	0.09	0.14	0.13	0.08	0.13	0.13	0.14	0.11	0.13	0.08	0.09	0.12	0.13	0.14	0.11	0.09
Food, beverages, and tobacco	0.13	0.09	0.13	0.12	0.08	0.13	0.10	0.14	0.11	0.14	0.07	0.05	0.13	0.12	0.08	0.08	0.09
Basic metals	0.25	—	0.17	0.18	—	—	0.18	—	—	0.10	0.10	0.14	0.11	0.24	0.27	0.16	0.08
Fragmented high-R&D industries:	0.16	0.12	0.13	0.13	0.11	0.15	0.17	0.17	0.12	0.16	0.09	0.11	0.06	0.13	0.09	0.13	0.10
Machinery and equipment	0.19	0.20	0.16	0.13	0.09	—	0.17	0.19	0.12	0.15	0.08	0.11	0.08	0.15	0.09	0.13	—
Other manufacturing and recycling	0.09	0.06	0.08	0.16	0.15	0.15	0.17	0.13	0.13	0.17	0.11	0.11	-0.05	0.10	0.09	—	0.10
Segmented high-R&D industries:	0.13	0.09	0.12	0.13	0.11	0.14	0.18	0.12	0.11	0.14	0.10	0.13	0.03	0.12	0.14	0.12	0.13
Chemical, plastics, rubber, and fuel products	0.11	0.09	0.12	0.16	0.11	0.17	0.15	0.11	0.12	0.13	0.10	0.14	0.03	0.13	0.18	0.15	0.15
Electrical and optical equipment	0.15	—	0.14	0.13	0.12	—	0.22	0.15	0.13	0.17	0.13	0.12	—	0.09	0.12	0.12	—
Transport equipment	0.14	0.09	0.13	0.09	0.08	0.11	0.17	0.11	0.07	0.14	0.08	0.11	0.02	0.09	0.11	0.08	0.10
Nonmanufacturing[a]	0.28	0.20	0.20	0.25	0.25	—	0.27	0.26	0.16	0.38	0.26	0.32	0.02	0.24	0.26	0.17	0.19
Electricity, gas, and water supply	0.34	0.23	0.35	0.37	0.41	—	0.37	0.27	0.15	0.30	0.46	0.32	—	0.19	0.48	—	0.20
Wholesale and retail trade, repairs	0.28	—	0.16	0.12	0.28	—	0.25	0.25	0.16	0.45	—	—	0.24	0.30	0.24	—	0.14
Transport and storage	0.14	—	0.26	0.13	0.18	—	0.33	0.22	0.10	—	0.17	—	—	0.21	0.27	0.18	0.16
Post and telecommunications	0.20	—	0.35	0.38	0.24	—	0.36	0.40	0.21	—	0.32	—	—	0.26	0.29	—	0.28
Financial intermediation	0.37	—	0.14	0.18	0.35	—	0.34	0.20	0.21	0.32	0.27	—	0.21	0.33	0.34	—	0.25
Business services	0.27	—	—	0.44	0.20	—	0.19	0.28	—	—	0.16	—	0.19	0.12	0.16	0.14	0.20

Source: Høj et al. 2007, 43.

Note: — = not available; R&D = research and development. Figures are averages using sectoral production as weights. Weights are country specific.

a. Nonmanufacturing excludes construction, real estate activities, and personal services.

that cross-country policy differences in PMR explain cross-country differences in economic performance, while the macroeconomic effects are likely to be significant because PMR extends to more and more industries and to changes in general purpose regulation.

Competition in product markets is obviously stymied by overly strict regulation in product markets. We would therefore expect to see higher markups associated with less product regulation. Schiantarelli (2008) provides a review of cross-country experience that examines the effect of PMR and reform on markups, firm dynamics, investment, employment, innovation, productivity, and output growth. Specifically, PMR affects (1) the allocation of resources between sectors producing different goods; (2) the allocation of resources between firms with different productivity in each sector; (3) the productivity of existing firms; and (4) the pace of productivity growth by altering the incentives to innovate and by determining the speed with which new products and processes replace old ones (Schiantarelli 2008).

Schiantarelli (2008) reviews the theoretical literature on each of these four facets, highlighting the ambiguity and caveats that arise, particularly in the studies of innovation and PMR. For example, the introduction of PMR would be expected to reduce monopoly profits. As these provide one of the main incentives for innovative activity, particularly in the creative destruction models championed by Schumpeter (1942), PMR may adversely affect the desire to innovate. Empirical research in this area is critical to understanding the impact of PMR. The empirical results on the relationship between innovation and competition suggest an inverted U-shaped pattern whereby innovation is affected adversely by a very competitive or very monopolistic environment.[6]

Further lessons from the microeconometric studies suggest that greater competition has a positive effect on the level and growth of productivity;[7] but in cases where greater firm productivity results in the firm increasing its market share and the market becoming more concentrated, then productivity is biased downward.[8] However, where privatization is accompanied by regulatory reform, in particular for service sector firms, there are gains in productivity from increased competition. Other empirical studies have examined the dynamics of productivity by decomposing aggregate productivity growth in different components, such as a "within" component arising from productivity improvements in continuing firms; a "between" component due to the reallocation of resources between continuing firms; and a component due to entry and exit (Schiantarelli 2008). The results from these studies are mixed, depending on the level of decomposition used and the time frame. The following results are cited by Schiantarelli (2008):

1. Bartelsman, Haltiwanger, and Scarpetta (2004) find that the "within" component of labor productivity is the most important component for the developed and nontransition emerging countries.

2. Foster, Haltiwanger, and Krizan (2001) find that net entry, the third component, becomes important (and positive) only at a horizon of 5 to 10 years.
3. Bartelsman, Haltiwanger, and Scarpetta (2004) find that entry is more important in transition countries, while being negative in most OECD countries and in the nontransition emerging economies.
4. The "between" component empirical studies have had mixed results (Schiantarelli 2008).

Turning to the macroeconomic effects, Schiantarelli (2008) reviews the empirical studies examining the effects of PMR on macroeconomic performance, that is, investment, employment, innovation, productivity, and output growth. Most of the empirical studies reviewed employ a reduced-form approach whereby PMR is an explanatory variable—either directly or indirectly through intermediate variables such as markup or firms' entry, exit, or turnover rates—in equations for factor demand, productivity, or innovation (see table 1.2).

An Example Using the OECD PMR Indicators

The OECD indicators of PMR allow us to examine the relationship between competition as measured by markups and the rules and regulations that have the potential to reduce the strength of competition (Høj et al. 2007).[9] The indicators, which measure the degree to which policies promote or inhibit competition in product markets, were constructed initially in 1998; they were updated in 2003 (the indicators were extended to include employment protection legislation), and again in 2008 (the indicators were substantially revised and the economy-wide PMR was extended to include greater sectoral information than heretofore). The most recent revision, in 2011, witnessed a move from "most-favored nation tariffs" to "effectively applied tariffs" and the inclusion of the Foreign Direct Investment (FDI) Regulatory Restrictiveness Index.[10] The PMR indicators measure the economywide regulatory and market environments in 20 OECD countries in or around 1998, 2003, and 2008, and in 4 other OECD countries (Chile, Estonia, Israel, and Slovenia) as well as in Brazil, China, India, Indonesia, the Russian Federation, and South Africa in or around 2008. They are consistent across time and countries.

The structure of the PMR indicator system is shown in figure 1.2. It takes a bottom-up approach, where the indicators can be related to specific underlying policies (Conway et al. 2010). It summarizes a large number of formal rules and regulations that have a bearing on competition. Hence, it is an objective measure of the regulatory stance. The information is organized into 18 low-level indicators that are progressively aggregated into three broad regulatory areas:

• State control of business enterprises
• Legal and administrative barriers to entrepreneurship
• Barriers to international trade and investment

Table 1.2 Review of Studies Examining the Effect of PMR on Macroeconomic Outcomes

Effect of PMR on	Study	Focus	Data source	Results
Markup	Griffith and Harrison (2004)	Two-step approach: Effect of product market reforms on the level of rents[a] Effect of variations in the markup on factor accumulation R&D and productivity[b]	Fraser Institute (2002) index of ease of starting a new business, of price controls, of time spent with government bureaucracy, of average tariff rates, and of regulatory trade barriers; European Center of Enterprises with Public Participation; and the Eurostat Structural indicators on state aid, public procurement, and on percentage that is publicly advertised	Many of the indicators measuring tightness of regulation have a significant positive effect on markups.
Turnover	Cincera and Galgau (2005)	Two-step approach Effect of regulation on entry and exit of new firms Effect of entry and exit on factor demand and productivity	Dun and Bradstreet database on the number of entries and exits for 352 digit sectors for 9 OECD countries	Deregulation tends to be significantly associated with more entry and exit.
Turnover	Loayza, Oviedo, and Serven (2005)	Effect of firm turnover rates on productivity growth and its components	Harmonized data set on firm dynamics constructed by Bartelsman, Haltiwanger, and Scarpetta (2004) for 6 Latin American countries and 9 industrial economies	PMR slows down the reallocation of resources following a shock.
Entry/exit	Scarpetta et al. (2002)	Effect of regulation on entry	OECD firm-level database constructed from business registers or social security databases	For firms employing between 20 and 99 workers, PMR has a negative and significant effect on entry. For the 100 to 499 class, the effect is positive and significant
Entry/exit	Brandt (2004)	Effect of regulation on entry	OECD firm-level database constructed from business registers or social security databases	Barriers to entry coefficient are not significant; some evidence of regulatory and administrative opacity affects entry rates.

table continues next page

7

Table 1.2 Review of Studies Examining the Effect of PMR on Macroeconomic Outcomes *(continued)*

Effect of PMR on	Study	Focus	Data source	Results
Entry/exit	Klapper, Laeven, and Rajan (2004)	Effect of regulation on entry	Cross-country firm-level Amadeus data set to construct entry and exit rates for Western and Eastern European countries	Regulation reduces entry relative to the "normal" industry-specific rate one observes in the United States with low barriers to entry.
Investment	Alesina et al. (2005)[c]	Effect of regulation on investment (by focusing on investment in nonmanufacturing industries that have experienced changes in their regulatory framework)	Time-varying sector country-specific measures of regulation	A reduction in regulation, particularly if it affects barriers to entry, has a significant and sizable positive effect on the investment rate.
Employment	Fiori et al. (2007)[c]	Effect of regulation on service employment	Employment rate equation for the business sector in OECD countries, including country-specific constants and controlling for endogeneity of policies	Gains from reducing barriers to entry in product markets are higher when labor market policies are tight; domestic product market deregulation generates a decline in bargaining power of workers (by promoting deregulation of labor market/affecting union density and coverage).

table continues next page

Table 1.2 Review of Studies Examining the Effect of PMR on Macroeconomic Outcomes *(continued)*

Effect of PMR on	Study	Focus	Data source	Results
Factor demand	Griffith and Harrison (2004)[c]	Effect of regulation on factor demand (employment and investment) via markup	Not specified	Decrease in regulation leads to decrease in markup; markup is negatively and significantly related to employment and investment.
	Cincera and Galgau (2005)	Effect of regulation on factor demand (employment and investment) via entry	Not specified; instrumental variables used for entry/exit because of endogeneity	Entry is not a significant determinant of the growth in investment, while exit is associated with a significant decrease in the pace of capital accumulation; for employment growth, the effect is not significant.
Innovation[d]	Bassanini and Ernst (2002)	Effect of product and labor market regulation (domestic economic regulation, administrative regulation, and tariffs and nontariff barriers) on R&D intensity (relative to output)	18 manufacturing industries in 18 OECD countries	Nontariff barriers have a negative effect on R&D intensity positive differential effect for employment protection in high-tech industries relative to low-tech in centralized systems of industrial relations.
	Griffith and Harrison (2004)	Effect of PMR on R&D through changes in the markup	Not specified	Markup has a positive and significant effect on R&D.

table continues next page

9

Table 1.2 Review of Studies Examining the Effect of PMR on Macroeconomic Outcomes *(continued)*

Effect of PMR on	Study	Focus	Data source	Results
Productivity and output growth[e]	Nicoletti and Scarpetta (2003)	Effect of regulation on TFP growth	17 manufacturing and 6 service industries for 18 OECD countries	Some evidence of a positive effect of privatization and entry liberalization on TFP growth exists. Also evidence shows that entry barriers in manufacturing may affect the pace of technology absorption, especially for countries far from the world frontier.
	IMF (2004)	Effect of regulation on per capita GDP growth	15 developed countries with a maximum of five observations on growth rates calculated over 3-year averages	Both product market reform and trade reform have a positive and significant effect on growth, although it may take time for the full effects to be realized.
	Loayza, Oviedo, and Serven (2004)	Effect of product and labor market regulation on growth	Both developing and developed countries	A negative and significant direct effect of product and labor market regulation on growth; better governance reduces the negative effect of regulation; overall effect of regulation is sizable and negative for most developing countries; zero or mildly positive for most developed.

Source: Schiantarelli 2008.

Note: GDP = gross domestic product; IMF = International Monetary Fund; OECD = Organisation for Economic Co-operation and Development; PMR = product market regulation; R&D = research and development; TFP = total factor productivity.

a. As measured by the ratio between value added and the sum of labor and capital costs.

b. Product market reform is an instrument for markup.

c. Authors find a positive effect of deregulation on investment and employment in the service sector, but no evidence of a positive (or negative) effect for manufacturing.

d. Schiantarelli (2008) concludes that the macroeconomic studies are not supportive of a strong positive effect of lower regulation on direct input measures of firms' innovative activities. The evidence for manufacturing is sensitive to country selection in the sample.

e. Most of the evidence points toward a positive effect of less stringent regulation on productivity growth; the effect of deregulation is larger in more developed countries, while better governance appears to mitigate the negative effects of regulation (Schiantarelli 2008).

Figure 1.2 The Tree Structure of the Economy-wide PMR Indicator

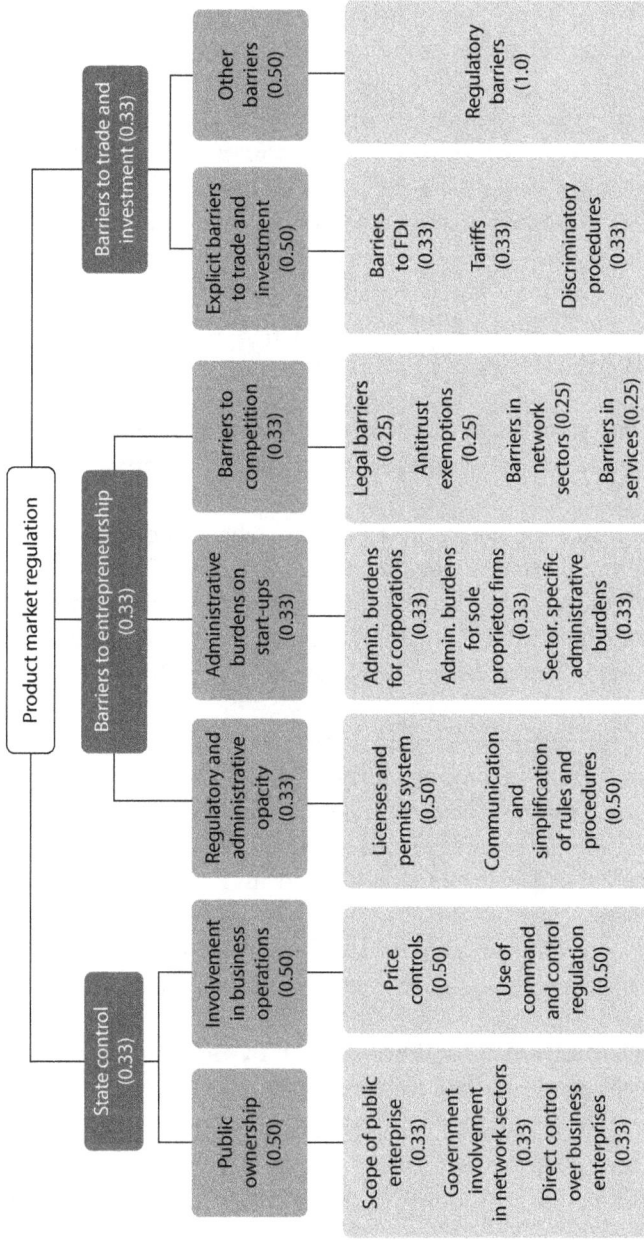

Source: Wölfl et al. 2010. © OECD. Used with permission; further permission required for reuse.
Note: FDI = foreign direct investment; PMR = product market regulation. Percentages in boxes refer to weights assigned.

The overall PMR indicator is a summary statistic of the general stance of PMR (Conway et al. 2010).

Wölfl et al. (2010) analyze the link between regulation (using the PMR) and growth for the OECD countries and non-OECD countries between 1998 and 2008. Their findings, based on growth regressions, suggest that less restrictive PMR is conducive to growth. For example, an improvement of 0.5 index points of barriers to entrepreneurship[11] would translate into approximately a 0.4 percent higher average annual rate of gross domestic product (GDP) per capita growth. However, the authors suggest that for less advanced countries, benefits arising from product market competition may be offset by other structural weaknesses. Thus, at early stages of industrial development, greater PMR (through, for example, some restrictions on foreign trade and investment) may be positive for growth.[12] The following results arise from the study by Wölfl et al. (2010):

1. Regulation is more restrictive of competition in accession countries,[13] enhanced engagement countries,[14] and non-OECD countries,[15] compared to OECD countries.
   a. Furthermore, regulation is most restrictive in enhanced engagement countries compared to most accession countries (see figure 1.3).
   b. Regulatory settings among Estonia, Slovenia, and Romania (non-OECD countries) are closer to those of the OECD average, compared to China, Russia, Israel, and Ukraine, where regulation is more restrictive.

2. Breaking down PMR into regulatory domains—state control, barriers to entrepreneurship, and barriers to trade and investment—suggests that the accession countries also face more restrictive regulation across all domains.
   a. Israel and Ukraine are characterized by restrictive regulation across the areas of state control, barriers to trade and investment, and barriers to entrepreneurship.
   b. Russia and Croatia also experience relatively high state control and barriers to trade and investment, and state control is relatively high in Bulgaria and Romania as well (see figure 1.4).
   c. Barriers to entrepreneurship and barriers to trade and investment in Chile, Estonia, Slovenia, Bulgaria, and Romania are at a level close to the OECD average.

3. The higher level of state control in enhanced engagement countries is due mainly to more widespread public control of business enterprises and a stronger use of coercive instead of incentive-based regulations. The higher overall barriers to entrepreneurship in India and Brazil are attributable largely to substantial red tape when setting up enterprises; in Indonesia, they are due to restricted entry in a large number of sectors. An onerous licensing and permits system characterizes the substantial barriers to entrepreneurship in South Africa.

Figure 1.3 PMR in Accession and OECD Countries, Aggregate Level, 2008

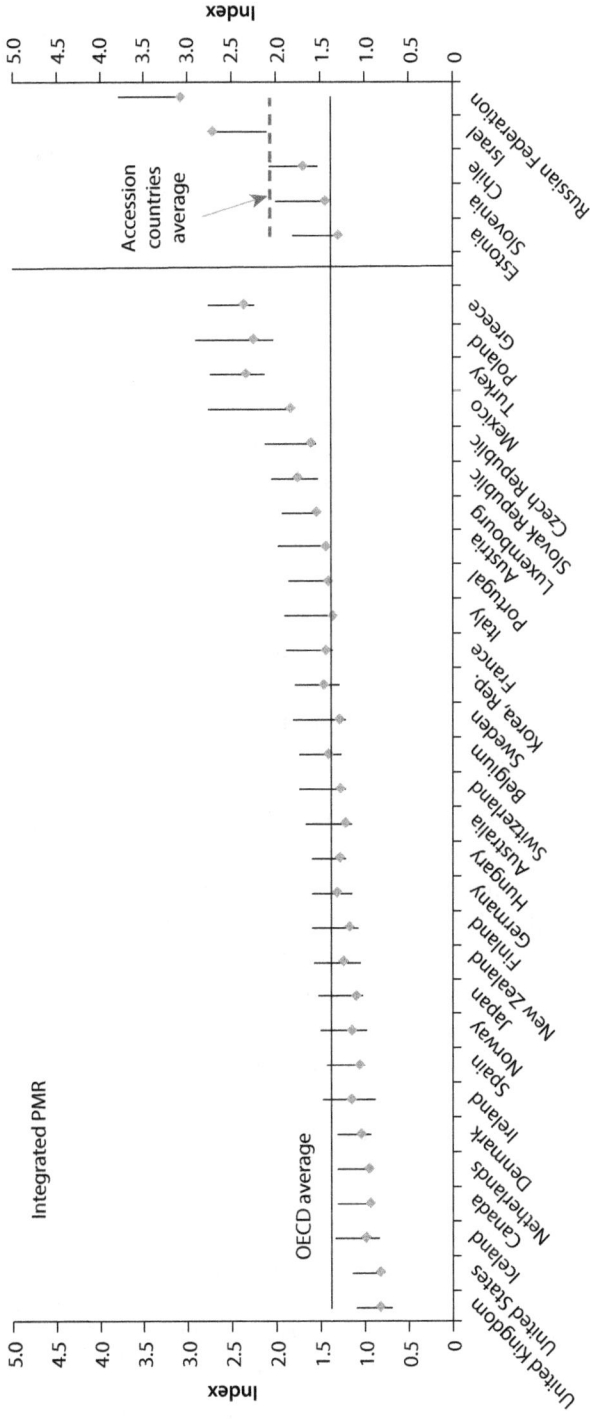

Source: Wölfl et al. 2010.

Note: OECD = Organisation for Economic Co-operation and Development; PMR = product market regulation. Figures are based on the "integrated" PMR indicator. Indicator values refer to one particular year and may no longer reflect the current regulatory stance in some (fast-reforming) countries. Confidence intervals are 90 percent and based on the random-weights approach. Index points are from 0 to 5 (least to most restrictive).

Figure 1.4 Decomposition of PMR in Accession Countries, 2008

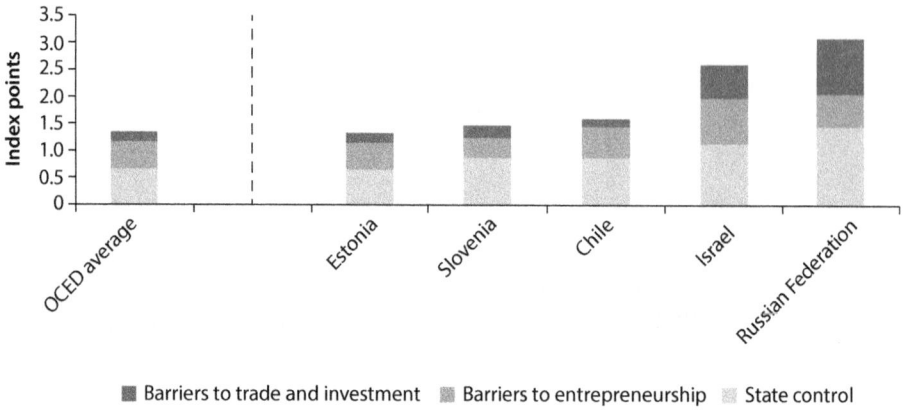

Legend: ■ Barriers to trade and investment   ■ Barriers to entrepreneurship   ▦ State control

Source: Wölfl et al. 2010.

Note: Based on the "integrated" product market regulation (PMR) indicator. Indicator values refer to one particular year and may no longer reflect the current regulatory stance in some (fast-reforming) countries. Index points are from 0 to 3.5 (least to most restrictive). The Organisation for Economic Co-operation and Development (OECD) average is a simple average.

Wölfl et al. (2010) investigate the relationship between PMR and growth in GDP per capita for 1998–2007 and for two subperiods, 1998–2003 and 2003–2007. The hypothesis is that PMRs impact economic growth, as summarized by the following equation:

$$y = \alpha + \beta * \mathrm{PMR} + \delta * X + \varepsilon,$$

where y is the average annual GDP growth rate per person aged 16–64 over a particular time period; PMR is the PMR indicator at different levels of disaggregation; and X is a matrix of control variables. Table 1.3 shows the results from the growth regression for the cross-section of countries over the entire time period and the cross-section over the two nonoverlapping subperiods.

The results are in line with cross-sectional growth regressions featuring conditional convergence in GDP per capita at an implied rate of 1.6 percent and the expected coefficients for investment (Wölfl et al. 2010). However, population growth and human capital are not significant in any of the three regressions—a fact that Wölfl et al. (2010, 20) attribute to the "smaller heterogeneity in terms of population growth and human capital among the countries in the sample." Aggregate product market regulation, the PMR variable, affects growth in the cross-section for the entire period only, suggesting that those countries with relatively liberal regulation in 1998 grew faster in average GDP per capita over the subsequent decade. The coefficient estimate suggests that a reduction in the overall PMR by 0.5 index points would translate into a 0.3 percent higher average annual rate of growth of per capita GDP.

Disaggregating the PMR indicator into its component parts suggests that the indicator for barriers to entrepreneurship appears to be driving most of the

Table 1.3 Regulation and Growth in GDP per Capita, Aggregate PMR

	Cross-section analysis Dependent variable: Average growth in GDP per person aged 16–64, Period 1998–2007		Panel analysis Dependent variable: Average growth in GDP per person aged 16–64, Period 1998–2003 and 2003–2007	
	Coefficient	Post-inclusion probability	Coefficient	Post-inclusion probability
Ln(GDP per capita)	−0.016***	99.4	−0.011*	77.1
Ln(population growth)	−0.003	21.5	−0.005	21.9
Ln(investment/GDP ratio)	0.032**	95.9	0.035***	99.4
Secondary enrollment ratio	0.000	19.1	0.000	10.6
Ethnic fragmentation	−0.002	21.1	−0.001	8.8
Government consumption	0.000	26.8	0.000	8.5
Inflation	0.000	21.4	−0.001*	81.8
% of land area in tropics and subtropics	−0.033**	98.4	−0.031*	94.3
Rule of law	0.000	14.1	−0.005+	55.0
Domestic credit to private sector	0.000	26.6	0.000	46.5
Crisis dummy			−0.018	48.3
PMR	−0.006*	79.7	−0.003	45.5
Observations	43		86	

Source: Wölfl et al. 2010.
Note: GDP = gross domestic product; PMR = product market regulation. Bayesian model averaging (BMA) techniques have been applied to the Barro type growth regression. BMA accommodates both a relatively large number of controls and a small number of observations and accounts for the so-called model uncertainty associated with the process of selecting the control variables. The variables chosen in the BMA here are standard variables used in growth regressions based on country samples that cover countries of different levels of development (Wölfl et al. 2010, 20). Constant always included but not reported. +Posterior inclusion probability ≥ 50 and < 75; *posterior inclusion probability ≥ 75 and ≤ 95; **posterior inclusion ≥ 95 and ≤ 99; ***posterior inclusion ≥ 99. The posterior model probability can be viewed as a measure of the relative data fit. In summing over all models that contain a particular regressor, the posterior inclusion probability of that regressor can be obtained. This statistic provides a probability measure of how important a regressor is to explain the dependent variable.

correlation between PMR and growth.[16] Furthermore, barriers to entrepreneurship are also significant in the panel regression (see table 1.4). The estimated coefficient on the entrepreneurship indicator for the entire time period suggests that an improvement of 0.5 index points would translate into a higher average annual rate of GDP per capita—between 0.35 percent and 0.4 percent—over the subsequent decade (Wölfl et al. 2010).

Disaggregating the barriers to entrepreneurship variable further—into regulatory and administrative capacity, administrative burdens on start-ups, and barriers to competition—"indicates that the link between barriers to entrepreneurship and growth is due mainly to the sub-domain 'barriers to competition'—which captures legal barriers to entry and antitrust exemptions" (Wölfl et al. 2010, 23).[17]

Wölfl et al. (2010) also examine the relationship between PMR and the level of economic development. Their main line of inquiry is whether the role of PMR differs for countries with different levels of development. They cite Acemoglu, Aghion, and Zilibotti (2006) and Aghion and Howitt (2005), who argued that countries that are less developed may benefit from policies that both foster capital deepening and introduce product market rigidities, especially

Table 1.4 Regulation and Growth in GDP per Capita, Regulatory Domains

	Cross-section analysis Dependent variable: Average growth in GDP per person aged 16–64, Period 1998–2007		Panel analysis Dependent variable: Average growth in GDP per person aged 16–64, Period 1998–2003 and 2003–2007	
	Coefficient	Post-inclusion probability	Coefficient	Post-inclusion probability
Ln(GDP per capita)	−0.016***	99.8	−0.014*	89.7
Ln(population growth)	−0.002	14.5	−0.003	14.0
Ln(investment/GDP ratio)	0.031**	96.7	0.033**	98.7
Secondary enrollment ratio	0.000	18.7	0.000	9.8
Ethnic fragmentation	−0.004	34.4	−0.001	8.3
Government consumption	0.000	30.1	0.000	8.0
Inflation	0.000	15.1	−0.001*	81.1
% of land area in tropics and subtropics	−0.028**	98.3	−0.031**	96.9
Rule of law	0.000	9.6	−0.003	38.1
Domestic credit to private sector	0.000	14.5	0.000	40.6
Crisis dummy			−0.018+	50.0
State control	0.000	17.6	0.000	9.2
Barriers to entrepreneurship	−0.008*	94.4	−0.007*	81.5
Barriers to trade and investment	0.000	17.2	0.000	9.6
Observations	43		86	

Source: Wölfl et al. 2010, 22.

Note: GDP = gross domestic product; PMR = product market regulation. Bayesian model averaging (BMA) techniques have been applied to the Barro type growth regression. BMA accommodates both a relatively large number of controls and a small number of observations and accounts for the so-called model uncertainty associated with the process of selecting the control variables. The variables chosen in the BMA here are standard variables used in growth regressions based on country samples that cover countries of different levels of development (Wölfl et al. 2010, 20). Constant always included but not reported. +Posterior inclusion probability ≥ 50 and < 75; *posterior inclusion probability ≥ 75 and ≤ 95; **posterior inclusion ≥ 95 and ≤ 99; ***posterior inclusion ≥ 99. The posterior model probability can be viewed as a measure of the relative data fit. In summing over all models that contain a particular regressor, the posterior inclusion probability of that regressor can be obtained. This statistic provides a probability measure of how important a regressor is to explain the dependent variable.

in relation to foreign competitors. The suggestion is that for low levels of GDP per capita, PMR may not have any effect on growth or may indeed have positive effects.

Two different methods are used by Wölfl et al. (2010) to test for differences in the effects of regulation on growth. The results from the second method, using a threshold approach based on Hansen (1999), are shown in table 1.5. Three separate regimes are identified based on initial GDP per capita, and the aggregate PMR measure is significantly negatively correlated with GDP per capita growth for middle- and high-income groups, especially the latter[18] (see table 1.5). The significant, positive correlation for the low-income regime suggests that some regulation may be advantageous for the low-income countries. Looking at the disaggregated PMR measure, barriers to entrepreneurship account for the large negative relationship between regulation and growth for the high-income countries, while barriers to trade and investment appear important for the low-income sample. The significant negative coefficient on trade barriers for the middle-income sample of countries suggests that trade barriers curb growth as development proceeds.

Table 1.5 Regulation and Growth in GDP per Capita, Threshold Results

	Panel analysis Dependent variable: Average growth in GDP per person aged 16–64, Period 1998–2003 and 2003–2007			
	Coefficient with aggregate PMR		Coefficient with regulatory domains	
Ln(GDP per capita)	0.006		−0.006	
Ln(investment/GDP ratio)	0.055***		0.036***	
Inflation	−0.001***		−0.001***	
% of land area in tropics and subtropics	−0.040***		−0.034***	
Domestic credit to private sector	0.000***			
Crisis dummy	−0.028			
PMR				
Low regime (lngdp per capita ≤ 9.6)	0.009***			
Middle regime (10 ≥ lngdp per capita > 9.6)	−0.006**			
High regime (lngdp per capita > 10)	−0.012***			
State control				
Low regime (lngdp per capita ≤ 9.6)			0.004	
Middle regime (10.25 ≥ lngdp per capita > 9.6)			0.001	
High regime (lngdp per capita ≤ 10.25)			−0.002	
Barriers to entrepreneurship				
Low regime (lngdp per capita ≤ 9.6)			−0.016	
Middle regime (10.25 ≥ lngdp per capita > 9.6)			0.007	
High regime (lngdp per capita > 10.25)			−0.008**	
Barriers to trade and investment				
Low regime (lngdp per capita ≤ 9.6)			0.014**	
Middle regime (10.25 ≥ lngdp per capita > 9.6)			−0.013***	
High regime (lngdp per capita > 10.25)			0.002	
Memorandum:	LR stat.	p-value	LR stat.	p-value
H0: linear vs H1: 2. regime model	16.342	0	7.661	0
H0: 1 regime vs H1: 3. regime model	3.532	0	9.492	0
R^2 adj.	0.65		0.61	
Observations	86		86	

Source: Wölfl et al. 2010.
Note: GDP = gross domestic product; PMR = product market regulation. Constant always included but not reported. Standard errors are in parenthesis. P-values are bootstrapped. For details, see Hansen (1999).
Significance level: * = 10 percent, ** = 5 percent, *** = 1 percent.

State control does not appear to have any effect on growth, independent of development. These results agree with the findings from the first method (Wölfl et al. 2010).

Summary

There are a number of data sets that provide information on PMR (see note 8). The conclusions that emerge from a review of the data sets are these:

• Regulatory burdens vary widely across the world, with regulation in poorer countries more stringent than in richer countries, and greater in countries with a French legal origin or with a socialist legal origin than in others.

- The dispersion of regulatory regimes is greater in developing countries relative to developed countries.
- There has been a generalized tendency toward the relaxation of regulation concerning entry, accompanied by a decrease in tariff and nontariff barriers to trade in manufacturing.
- Many developing countries, including India and China, have been moving toward less restrictive regulation.
- OECD countries have experienced substantial deregulation in services and in sectors such as telecommunications, utilities, and transport.
- Regulatory reform began first in the United States in the early 1980s. The United Kingdom, Canada, New Zealand, and the Nordic European countries started to reform in the mid-1980s, whereas Australia and other European countries began market reform in the mid-1990s.
- Regulatory reform has often been accompanied by privatization, so that there has been a tendency for the share of output produced by public enterprises to decrease (Schiantarelli 2008).

Competition Policy

Effective competition does not happen automatically. Competition may be harmed by vested interests, inappropriate government policies, and anticompetitive behavior of incumbent firms. Ellis and Singh (2010a, 4) write that "appropriate policies are crucial to create the conditions within which competition can thrive, and competition authorities can help to build a culture of competition, and increase awareness of competition issues amongst policy makers and the public." Competition policy extends to all policies that generate an environment in which competition can flourish. Other government policies with a bearing on competition are trade policy, regulation, privatization, industrial policy, and competition law. Implementing and maintaining an effective competition framework is critical for attracting investment and developing the private sector (Ellis 2008; Godfrey 2008; Broadman 2007). Competition policies must be cognizant of a country's developmental standing and its governance capacities. This approach, while promoting the concept of competition, prevents the adoption of a one-size-fits-all model and the pursuit of "maximum competition" that may be harmful to socioeconomic development. Competition policy is a prime part of an economy's development strategy. It is of particular importance to developing economies in this era of globalization and liberalization.

Research on the state of competition in most developing economies is stymied by a lack of sufficient data and difficulty in attributing outcomes to competition policy per se (especially where competition reform was part of a package of economic reform). Nevertheless, globalization and the liberalization of developing country economies provide compelling arguments for competition policies. The enormous structural and regulatory changes that have occurred in developing economies over the last few decades as a result of privatization and deregulation require an appropriate competition policy to ensure improved economic performance. For example, replacing a privatized public natural monopoly with a privatized private sector monopoly is not good for social welfare. Singh (2002) suggests that ownership is not the issue, but rather the extent of competition, which depends on the external environment. The unprecedented activity in mergers and acquisitions that took place in the 1990s has reshaped the world economy and provides another "important reason for developing countries to have competition laws" (Singh 2002, 9). Singh (2002) outlines the concerns for developing countries. One direct effect is the increased market power of large multinationals and their potential abuse of dominance, such as by acquiring domestic firms. The developing country may be affected indirectly as a result of the reduced contestability of the market owing to the few large players. Competition law would help restrain cartels and other uncompetitive conduct by large multinationals. However, the success of competition law relies upon an adequately developed institutional and legal framework.

Developing economies present many challenges and opportunities to the implementation of effective competition policy. For many firms, in particular large firms, competitive success is tied to the government. The existence of an economic elite with close ties to the government prevents the development of competition policy (Ellis 2008). Breaking down the barriers that protect this elite is the focus of competition policy. Competition authorities have a role to play in mobilizing interest groups to lobby for reform. Interest groups are those that stand to gain from reforms, such as households, industrial consumers, and potential new entrants. On the other hand, competition policy can facilitate a level playing field for small and medium enterprises. Many of the poor in developing economies are small entrepreneurs, including farmers. They stand to benefit from an improved competitive environment in which entry and exit barriers are low, inputs are priced fairly, and opportunities exist for selling output at fair and competitive prices (Godfrey 2008).

Godfrey (2008) refers to a database on media allegations of anticompetitive behavior in Sub-Saharan Africa for the 10 years ending December 2004 that revealed a number of competition concerns in the region. Concerns arose from anticompetitive practices in the sugar and flour industries, in the prices of manufacturing inputs, and in the output markets for cotton, tea, coffee, and tobacco. Aghion, Braun, and Fedderke (2006) found that markups are significantly higher in manufacturing industries in South Africa compared to manufacturing industries worldwide. Broadman (2007) compared the administrative barriers to starting a business across a number of developing regions and found that these were significantly more onerous in Sub-Saharan Africa (table 1.6).

More recently, Ellis and Singh (2010b) examined the extent of competition for four markets in five developing economies from Africa and Asia. Table 1.7 shows the details.

Table 1.6 Administrative Barriers to Starting a Business, by Region

Starting a business	Sub-Saharan Africa	East Asia	South Asia
Number of procedures	11.0	8.2	7.9
Time in days	63.8	52.6	35.3
Cost (% per capita income)	215.3	42.9	40.5
Minimum capital (% per capita income)	297.2	109.2	0.8

Source: Broadman 2007, cited in Godfrey 2008.

Ellis and Singh (2010b) conclude the following from their case studies:

1. Markets with more competition, more players, more dynamic entry and exit, and more intense rivalry for customers tend to deliver better market outcomes.
2. Competition is often constrained—some industries by their nature are highly concentrated (cement and beer, for example)—but competition authorities have an important role to play in monitoring, publicizing, and tackling anti-competitive behavior.
3. The state has a large role in determining competition and market outcomes, through regulation, state ownership and privatization, price controls or subsidization, import protection, industrial policy, corrupt business deals, and ownership by individual politicians or their families.
4. In some countries and markets, there is a close relationship between government and business that creates a powerful economic elite with vested interests in opposing procompetition, progrowth reforms.

Singh (2002) examines the evidence for competition and competition policy in emerging markets after the Asian financial crisis. He finds, contrary to opinion, that competition in the more advanced emerging markets is just as intense as in advanced economies. An example of this finding is shown in table 1.8, which compares the persistence of profitability as measured by the time series estimates of persistence coefficients. The coefficients are lower for developing economies compared to advanced economies, suggesting that the developing economies are "subject to no less, if not greater competition, than advanced countries" (Singh 2002, 4). Moreover, Singh suggests that competition among small enterprises in the emerging markets is more intense than in advanced economies. Tybout (2000) reviewed the empirical evidence on competition in emerging markets and suggested that the evidence did not support the view that manufacturing plants and jobs had lower turnover rates in emerging markets than in OECD countries.

Competition policy in developing economies was formulated and implemented over the last three decades—just 16 developing economies had a formal competition policy before 1990—with 50 countries completing legislation for competition laws in the 1990s and a further 27 in the early 2000s (Singh 2002). The relative absence of competition policy was easily

Table 1.7 Structure, Conduct, and Performance of Selected Industries in Five Developing Economies

	Sugar		Cement		Beer		Mobile telephony	
	Ownership	Notes	Ownership	Notes	Ownership	Notes	Ownership	Notes
Bangladesh	State	Low productivity; poor performance; obsolete technology; inefficient farming methods	Many different market players	Greater evidence of price and nonprice competition	Highly concentrated	No further information	Relatively competitive	Lowest tariffs across five countries; regulated price floor is a concern— putting smaller operators and new entrants at a disadvantage
Kenya	State	Struggling to compete with private producers domestically and internationally	Very concentrated	Competition authority is investigating issue of joint ownership among three suppliers	Highly concentrated	Many anticompetitive practices identified— territorial allocation, price fixing, exclusive dealership	Relatively concentrated until recently	Entry of two new players has coincided with a fall in tariffs by 50 percent
Vietnam	State	Need substantial levels of costly government subsidization	Many different suppliers	Greater evidence of price and nonprice competition	Least concentrated of five countries; seven producers	Prices are lowest; nonprice competition seems strongest, but there are allegations of exclusive dealing, abuse of dominance	Mainly state	Operators appear to compete fiercely

table continues next page

Table 1.7 Structure, Conduct, and Performance of Selected Industries in Five Developing Economies *(continued)*

	Sugar		Cement		Beer		Mobile telephony	
	Ownership	Notes	Ownership	Notes	Ownership	Notes	Ownership	Notes
Zambia	Private	Produces highest amounts of sugar per hectare of five countries; Profitable, internationally competitive industry, domestic sugar prices are high; Monopolistic market structure	Very concentrated	Competition authority investigating supply constraints; Price of cement has fallen by almost 10 percent since 2008, coinciding with new market player in 2009	Monopoly producer	Highest prices of five countries; competition authority has imposed conditions; Evidence of barriers to entry, resale price maintenance, and exclusive dealership	State	Lowest mobile penetration rate; highest prices; government-controlled gateway that charges high prices to private operators
Ghana	Two potential entrants	State-led sugar industry collapsed; country now imports all sugar. Two entrants looking for government guarantees against imports	Two suppliers	Allegations of price hikes not investigated due to absence of competition authority	Two firms	Allegations of price leadership; prices are low, suggesting fierce competition	Two operators	Intense competition; good mobile penetration; relatively low prices; effective regulator

Source: Ellis and Singh 2010b.

Table 1.8 Persistence of Profitability in Emerging Markets and Advanced Markets

Emerging market country	Score	Source	Advanced market country	Score	Source
Brazil	0.013	Glen, Lee, and	Canada	0.425	Khemani and Shapiro (1990)
India	0.229	Singh (2001)	France	0.142	
Korea, Republic of	0.323		Germany	0.410	
Malaysia	0.349		Germany	0.485	Schwalbach, Grasshof, and Mahmood (1989)
Mexico	0.222		Germany	0.509	Schohl (1990)
Zimbabwe	0.421		Japan	0.465	Odagiri and Yamawaki (1990)
			United Kingdom	0.482	Cubbin and Geroski (1990)
			United Kingdom	0.488	Geroski and Jacquemin (1988)
			United States	0.183	Mueller (1990)
			United States	0.540	Waring (1996)

Source: Singh 2002.

understood in the developing economy context, in which there was considerable state control over industry. The government intervened directly when it perceived any anticompetitive behavior and fixed prices for other essential products (Singh 2002). A World Bank (2002) survey of competition laws identified intercountry differences along three key dimensions of competition law: the definition of dominance, the treatment of cartels, and enforcement.

The Competition Assessment Framework (CAF) was designed by the U.K. Department for International Development (DFID 2008) to identify and assess the nature of anticompetitive practices.[19] It was designed for policy makers in developing economies to "provide guidance on how a sector-by-sector approach to the state of competition can be undertaken" (Godfrey 2008, 8). It is applicable to all country situations, from a functioning competition authority, sector regulators, and competition law to the absence of all of these. It can help in formulating policy advice on the effects of anticompetitive practices in key markets, can inform the design of programs or projects to catalyze private sector development, and can serve as part of a holistic "growth diagnostic" (Godfrey 2008). A summary of the CAF as described by Godfrey (2008) is shown in table 1.9.

Singh (2002) suggests that a competition policy for a developing economy must be able to (1) restrain anticompetitive behavior by domestic privatized firms; (2) limit abuses of monopoly power by megacorporations created by the international merger movement; and (3) promote development. Singh (2002) is quite pessimistic about the ability of some developing countries to implement competition policy, in particular because competition policy requires a strong state that many developing countries lack. For developing economies with strong governments, even if not always democratic (for example, China, India, Brazil, and Mexico), he suggests a broad-based competition policy that would "in some

Table 1.9 Competition Assessment Framework

Themes	Questions	Notes
Selecting sectors and markets for assessment	Applying objective measures to select a sector for competition assessment, including its role in the economy, importance to consumers, concern about prices, past performance, entry barriers, and market concentration	Sector should be important to the economy; should be suggestive of competition problems
Identifying the relevant markets and the competitors	Questions to identify the relevant market or markets in the sector	Need to identify existing suppliers and buyers and their importance in the market
Examining the market structure	How to assess the level of concentration in the market	High concentration is often, although not exclusively a significant factor in market behavior
Looking for barriers to entry	Whether there are any significant barriers to entry	Questions examine natural barriers, strategic barriers, regulatory and policy barriers, and gender barriers
Ascertaining if government policies or institutions limit competition	Reviews the legislation, policies, and institutions of governments at all levels (national, state, local); questions seek to ascertain if state-owned enterprises receive any preferences that might restrict competition by the private sector	This may include licensing restrictions, FDI restrictions, and trade barriers
Considering vested interests	Questions seek to identify the objectives, power, and influence of stakeholders opposed to competition in a market	Sensitive area; vested interest may be personal, corporate, or institutional
Looking for signs of anticompetitive conduct by firms	Questions are aimed at identifying practices of firms that can impede competition; for example, abuse of dominance, collusion among competitors, and impact of M&A	Dominance is possible where a firm has strong market power arising from high market share and barriers to entry; cartels may be solely domestic firms or a mix of domestic and international; M&A may benefit or harm competition
Drawing conclusions	Review conclusions to each of the preceding and form a view on overall state of competition in each sector	Annexes to the CAF provide additional information on the definition of markets and calculation of market concentration

Source: Godfrey 2008.
Note: CAF = Competition Assessment Framework; FDI = foreign direct investment; M&A = mergers and acquisitions.

instances involve restriction of competition and in others its vigorous promotion" (2002, 16). Optimal competition rather than maximum competition should be the goal, with a blend of competition and cooperation designed to achieve sustained economic growth. As noted earlier, competition policy should not assume that one size fits all, but rather depend on the development stage of the underlying economy, as well as the effectiveness of its government and its institutional framework. In addition, he suggests that the private sector's propensity to invest be maintained at high levels and notes that the need for a steady growth of profits may necessitate governmental involvement in investment decisions (that is, to prevent overcapacity and falling profits). He highlights the crucial importance of industrial policy in achieving the structural changes needed for economic development; this role for industrial policy necessitates its coherence with competition policies (Singh 2008).

Conclusion

The chapter addressed two concepts—competition and competition policy. The degree and nature of competition in an economy have implications for growth. The chapter examined competition in product markets. Regulation in product markets suggests how supportive an economy is of competition. In principle, more stringent regulation is negatively associated with economic growth, while improved governance lessens the negative effects of regulation.

The first part of the chapter looked at PMR and economic performance, identifying the ambiguities and caveats that arise at the microeconomic, firm, and macroeconomic levels. In general, less restrictive PMR is conducive to growth. However, this relationship is dependent upon the level of development in the economy, and at early stages of development, greater PMR through restrictions on foreign trade and investment may be positive for growth. Regulation tends to be more stringent in developing economies, although many, including China and India, are moving toward less restrictive regulation.

The chapter then addressed the issue of competition policy, noting that effective competition does not happen automatically and highlighting the role of competition policy and other policies in establishing the appropriate environment for competition to thrive. Trade policy, regulation, privatization, industrial policy, and competition law all have a bearing on competition. Furthermore, competition policy needs to take into account an economy's developmental stage and its governance capabilities.

The chapter cited a number of reasons why competition policy is particularly important for developing economies. One has to do with the current era of globalization and liberalization. Furthermore, the success of the structural and regulatory changes that took place in developing economies following mass privatization and deregulation requires appropriate competition policies. The large-scale activity in mergers and acquisitions during the 1990s reshaped the world economy with implications for developing economies.

The chapter also presented some evidence for the extent of competition and competition policy in developing and emerging market economies. We concluded with a synopsis of the CAF that is supporting competition policy reform in India. It was designed to identify and assess the nature of anticompetitive practices and is helpful in formulating policy advice.

Notes

1. See Ahn (2002); Nickell (1996); Disney, Haskel, and Heden (2000); and Klette (1999), referenced in Yun (2004).
2. Increasing managerial effort may be in response to the risk of losing market share or to greater opportunities for comparing performance across firms; see Nickell (1996).

3. See Ahn (2002). Furthermore, Nicoletti et al. (2001), Bassanini and Ernst (2002), and Jaumotte and Pain (2005) suggest that "too strict and too high nontrade barriers are associated with low research and development (R&D) intensity in the business sector" (Høj et al. 2007, 6).

4. Alesina et al. (2005) find that procompetitive reforms increase capital deepening in nonmanufacturing industries. Nicoletti and Scarpetta (2003) find the same reforms considered by Alesina et al. (2005) improve multifactor productivity and facilitate a faster catch-up to the technological leader. Conway et al. (2006) find similar effects of competition on investment in information and communications technology and labor productivity growth (Høj et al. 2007).

5. The two dimensions and four groups of manufacturing industries classification derive from Oliveira Martins, Price, and Mulder (2002). The authors mapped manufacturing sectors into this twofold classification using an estimate of the minimum efficient scale to determine which markets/industries were fragmented or segmented and R&D intensity to classify industries according to the level of endogenous sunk costs.

6. See Blundell, Griffith, and Van Reenen (1999) and Aghion et al. (2005).

7. The paper by Nickell (1996) is seminal in this area. Its findings were confirmed by Disney, Haskel, and Heden (2000).

8. This is found in Nickell (1996) for U.K. firm data, in Klette (1999) for Norwegian plant data, and in Bottasso and Sembenelli (2001) for Italian firm data.

9. The product market regulation (PMR) is just one data series. Other data series that facilitate an examination of PMR are the Eurostat data on sectoral and ad hoc state aid, public procurement, and openly advertised public procurement; data from the European Centre for Public Enterprises with Public Participation (CEEP); the World Bank Doing Business Indicators database, available at http://www.doingbusiness.org; the World Bank Investment Climate Assessment survey; and data on the effect of regulation collected by the Fraser Institute (Schiantarelli 2008).

10. The Foreign Direct Investment (FDI) restrictiveness index, originally developed in 2003, measures the restrictiveness of a given country's policy toward FDI on a scale of 0 (no restrictions) to 1 (no FDI). Four types of measures are covered: (1) foreign equity restrictions; (2) screening and prior approval requirements; (3) rules for key personnel; and (4) other restrictions on the operation of foreign enterprises. The index covers 22 sectors, the scores for which are averaged to obtain a country score: the FDI index for the country concerned. The index is available for all Organisation for Economic Co-operation and Development (OECD) members, adherents to the Declaration on International Investment and Multinational Enterprises, enhanced engagement countries, and other G-20 countries (Kalinova, Palerm, and Thomsen 2010).

11. Empirical studies suggest that the correlation between procompetitive policies and growth is driven largely by factors that promote entrepreneurship and competition. Thus, the "barriers to entrepreneurship" variable is the one considered.

12. See also Acemoglu, Aghion, and Zilibotti (2006) and Aghion and Howitt (2005).

13. The accession countries in the study are Chile, Estonia, Israel, Russia, and Slovenia.

14. Enhanced engagement countries are Brazil, China, India, Indonesia, and South Africa.

15. Nonmember OECD countries in this study are Bulgaria, Croatia, Romania, and Ukraine.

16. The insignificance of the state control variable agrees with results from the empirical literature that suggest that privatization can bear fruit only if it is combined with

liberalization. An insignificant "barriers to trade and investment" variable may reflect underlying country differences caused by countries' different stages of economic development (Wölfl et al. 2010).

17. Wölfl et al. (2010) urge caution when "interpreting these results as the sub-domains are highly correlated in [this] small sample."

18. Countries in the low regime include Brazil, Bulgaria, China, India, Indonesia, Romania, Russia, South Africa, Turkey, and Ukraine. Countries in the middle regime include Chile, Croatia, Estonia, Hungary, Republic of Korea, Mexico, Poland, and, the Slovak Republic. Countries in the high regime are Australia, Austria, Belgium, Canada, the Czech Republic, Denmark, Finland, France, Germany, Greece, Iceland, Ireland, Italy, Japan, Luxembourg, New Zealand, Netherlands, Norway, Portugal, Slovenia, Spain, Sweden, Switzerland, the United Kingdom, and the United States.

19. "The CAF was designed in response to demand from the current DFID/FIAS (UK Department of International Development/Foreign Investment Advisory Service at the World Bank) program that is supporting competition policy reform in India" (Godfrey 2008, 8).

References

Acemoglu, D., P. Aghion, and F. Zilibotti. 2006. "Distance to Frontier, Selection, and Economic Growth." *Journal of the European Economic Association* 4 (1): 37–74.

Aghion, P., N. Bloom, R. Blundell, R. Griffith, and P. Howitt. 2005. "Competition and Innovation: An Inverted-U Relationship." *Quarterly Journal of Economics* 20 (2): 701–28.

Aghion, P., M. Braun, and J. Fedderke. 2006. "Competition and Productivity Growth in South Africa." Working Paper No. 132, Center for International Development at Harvard University, Cambridge, MA.

Aghion, P., and P. Howitt. 2005. "Appropriate Growth Policy: A Unifying Framework." Joseph Schumpeter Lecture. *Journal of the European Economic Association* 4 (4): 269–314.

Ahn, S. 2002. "Competition, Innovation and Productivity Growth: A Review of Theory and Evidence." Economics Department Working Paper 317, Organisation for Economic Co-operation and Development, Paris, France.

Alesina, A., S. Ardagna, G. Nicoletti, and F. Schiantarelli. 2005. "Regulation and Investment." *Journal of the European Economic Association* 3 (4): 791–825.

Bartelsman, E., J. Haltiwanger, and S. Scarpetta. 2004. "Microeconomic Evidence of Creative Destruction in Industrial and Developing Countries." World Development Report background Paper, World Bank, Washington, DC.

Bassanini, A., and E. Ernst. 2002. "Labour Market Institutions, Product Market Regulation, and Innovation: Cross-country Evidence." Economics Department Working Paper 316, Organisation for Economic Co-operation and Development, Paris, France.

Blundell, R., R. Griffith, and J. Van Reenen. 1999. "Market Share, Market Value and Innovation in a Panel of British Manufacturing Firms." *Review of Economic Studies* 66: 529–54.

Bottasso, A., and A. Sembenelli. 2001. "Market Power, Productivity, and the EU Single Market Program: Evidence from a Panel of Italian Firms." *European Economic Review* 45 (1): 167–86.

Brandt, N. 2004. "Business Dynamics, Regulation and Performance." OECD Directorate for Science Technology and Industry Working Paper 2004/3, Organisation for Economic Co-operation and Development, Paris, France.

Broadman, H. 2007. *Africa's Silk Road: China and India's New Economic Frontier.* Washington, DC: World Bank.

Cincera, M., and O. Galgau. 2005. "Impact of Market Entry and Exit on EU Productivity and Growth Performance." European Economy Economic Paper 222, Directorate General Economic and Monetary Affairs, European Commission, Brussels, Belgium.

Conway, P., D. de Rosa, G. Nicoletti, and F. Steiner. 2006. "Regulation, Competition and Productivity Convergence." Economics Department Working Paper 509, Organisation for Economic Co-operation and Development, Paris, France.

Conway, P., R. Herd, T. Chalaux, P. He, and J. Yu. 2010. "Product Market Regulation and Competition in China." Economics Department Working Paper 823, Organisation for Economic Co-operation and Development, Paris, France.

Cubbin, J. S., and P. A. Geroski. 1990. "The Persistence of Profits in the United Kingdom." In *The Dynamics of Company Profits: An International Comparison,* edited by D. C. Mueller, 147–68. Cambridge, UK: Cambridge University Press.

DFID (Department for International Development). 2008. *Competition Assessment Framework: An Operational Guide for Identifying Barriers to Competition in Developing Countries.* London: DFID.

Disney, R., J. Haskel, and Y. Heden. 2000. "Restructuring and Productivity Growth in UK Manufacturing." Discussion Paper 2463, Centre for Economic Policy Research, London.

Ellis, K. 2008. "How to Achieve Growth: The Million-Dollar Question." ODI Opinion, Overseas Development Institute, London. http://www.odi.org.uk/sites/odi.org.uk/files/odi-assets/publications-opinion-files/820.pdf.

Ellis, K., and R. Singh. 2010a. "The Economic Impact of Competition." Project Briefing No. 42, Overseas Development Institute, London, UK.

———. 2010b. *Assessing the Economic Impact of Competition.* London: Overseas Development Institute. http://dspace.cigilibrary.org/jspui/bitstream/123456789/29339/1/Assessing%20the%20Economic%20Impact%20of%20Competition.pdf?1.

Fiori, G., G. Nicoletti, S. Scarpetta, and F. Schiantarelli. 2007. "Employment Outcomes and the Interaction between Product and Labor Market Deregulation: Are They Substitutes or Complements?" Department of Economics Working Paper 663, Boston College, Boston, MA.

Foster, L., J. Haltiwanger, and C. J. Krizan, 2001. "Aggregate Productivity Growth: Lessons from Microeconomic Evidence." In *New Developments in Productivity Analysis,* edited by C. Hulten, E. Dean, and M. Harper, 303–72. Chicago: University of Chicago Press.

Fraser Institute. 2002. *Economic Freedom of the World: 2002 Annual Report.* Vancouver: Fraser Institute.

Glen, J., K. Lee, and A. Singh. 2001. "Persistence of profitability and competition in emerging markets." *Economics Letters* 72: 247–53.

Geroski, P. A., and A. Jacquemin. 1988. "The Persistence of Profits: A European Comparison." *Economic Journal* 98: 375–89.

Godfrey, N. 2008. "Why Is Competition Important for Growth and Poverty Reduction?" Paper prepared for the Global Forum on International Investment VII, Paris, March 27–28. http://www.oecd.org/investment/globalforum/40315399.pdf.

Griffith, R., and R. Harrison. 2004. "The Link between Product Market Reform and Macro-economic Performance." European Economy Economic Paper 209, Directorate General Economic and Monetary Affairs, European Commission, Brussels, Belgium.

Hansen, B. 1999. "Threshold Effects in Non-dynamic Panels: Estimation, Testing, Interference." *Journal of Econometrics* 93 (2): 345–68.

Høj, J., M. Jimenez, M. Maher, G. Nicoletti, and M. Wise. 2007. "Product Market Competition in the OECD Countries: Taking Stock and Moving Forward." Economics Department Working Paper 575, Organisation for Economic Co-operation and Development, Paris, France.

Jaumotte, F., and N. Pain. 2005. "Innovation in the Business Sector." Economics Department Working Paper 459, Organisation for Economic Co-operation and Development, Paris, France.

Kalinova, B., A. Palerm, and S. Thomsen. 2010. "OECD's FDI Restrictiveness Index: 2010 Update." Working Paper on International Investment, No. 2010/3, Organisation for Economic Co-operation and Development Investment Division, Paris, France.

Khemani, R. S., and D. M. Shapiro. 1990. "The Persistence of Profitability in Canada." In *The Dynamics of Company Profits: An International Comparison*, edited by D. C. Mueller, 77–104. Cambridge, UK: Cambridge University Press.

Klapper, L., L. Laeven, and R. G. Rajan. 2004. "Business Environment and Firm Entry: Evidence from International Data." Working Paper 10380, National Bureau of Economic Research, Cambridge, MA.

Klette, T. J. 1999. "Market Power, Scale Economies and Productivity: Estimates from a Panel of Establishment Data." *Journal of Industrial Economics* 47 (4): 451–76.

Loayza, N. V., A. M. Oviedo, and L. Serven. 2004. "Regulation and Macroeconomic Performance." Working Paper, World Bank, Washington, DC.

———. 2005. "Regulation and Microeconomic Dynamics: A Comparative Assessment for Latin America." Working Paper, World Bank, Washington, DC.

Mueller, D. C., ed. 1990. *The Dynamics of Company Profits: An International Comparison*. Cambridge, UK: Cambridge University Press.

Nickell, S. 1996. "Competition and Corporate Performance." *Journal of Political Economy* 104: 724–46.

Nicoletti, G., A. Bassanini, E. Ernst, S. Jean, P. Santiago, and P. Swaim. 2001. "Product and Labor Market Interactions in OECD Countries." Economics Department Working Paper 226, Organisation for Economic Co-operation and Development, Paris, France.

Nicoletti, G., and S. Scarpetta. 2003. "Regulation, Productivity and Growth: OECD Evidence." *Economic Policy* 18 (36): 11–72.

———. 2005. "Product Market Reforms and Employment in OECD Countries." Economics Department Working Paper 472, Organisation for Economic Co-operation and Development, Paris, France.

Odagiri, H., and H. Yamawaki. 1990. "The Persistence of Profits in Japan." In *The Dynamics of Company Profits: An International Comparison*, edited by D. C. Mueller, 169–86. Cambridge, UK: Cambridge University Press.

OECD (Organisation for Economic Co-operation and Development). 2002. "Product Market Competition and Economic Performance." *OECD Economic Outlook* 2: 155–62.

Oliveira Martins, J., T. Price, and N. Mulder. 2002. "A Taxonomy of Market Cluster." Mimeo, Organisation for Economic Co-operation and Development, Paris.

Scarpetta, S., P. Hemmings, T. Tressel, and J. Woo. 2002. "The Role of Policy and Institutions for Productivity and Firm Dynamics: Evidence from Micro and Industry Data." Economics Department Working Paper 329, Organisation for Economic Co-operation and Development, Paris, France.

Schiantarelli, F. 2008. "Product Market Regulation and Macroeconomic Performance: A Review of Cross-country Evidence." Working Paper, Boston College, Boston. http://fmwww.bc.edu/ec-p/wp623.pdf.

Schohl, F. 1990. "Persistence of Profits in the Long Run: A Critical Extension of Some Recent Findings." *International Review of Industrial Organization* 8: 385–403.

Schumpeter, J. A. 1942. *Capitalism, Socialism and Democracy.* New York: Harper and Brothers.

Schwalbach, J., U. Grasshof, and T. Mahmood. 1989. "The Dynamics of Corporate Profits." *European Economic Review* 3: 1625–39.

Singh. A. 2002. "Competition and Competition Policy in Emerging Markets: International and Developmental Dimensions." Research Papers for the Intergovernmental Group of Twenty-Four on International Monetary Affairs, G-24 Discussion Paper 18, United Nations, New York.

_____. 2008. "The Past, Present, and Future of Industrial Policy in India: Adapting to the Changing Domestic and International Environment." Working Paper No. 376, ESCRC Centre for Business Research, University of Cambridge, Cambridge, U.K.

Tybout, J. 2000. "Manufacturing Firms in Developing Countries: How Well Do They Do, and Why?" *Journal of Economic Literature* 38: 11–44.

Waring, G. 1996. "Industry Differences in the Persistence of Firm-specific Returns." *American Economic Review* 86: 1253–265.

Wölfl, A., I. Wanner, O. Röhn, and G. Nicoletti. 2010. "Product Market Regulation: Extending the Analysis beyond OECD Countries." Economics Department Working Paper 799, Organisation for Economic Co-operation and Development, Paris, France.

World Bank. 2002. *World Development Report: Building Institutions for Markets.* Washington, DC: World Bank and Oxford University Press.

Yun, M. 2004. "Competition and Productivity Growth: Evidence from Korean Manufacturing Firms." In *Competition, Competitiveness and Development: Lessons from Developing Countries*, UNCTAD/DITC/CLP/2004/1, United Nations Conference on Trade and Development, Geneva. http://unctad.org/en/Docs/ditcclp20041ch4_en.pdf.

CHAPTER 2

Competitiveness and Its Indicators

Competitiveness is a broad concept applied at many different levels and measured by many different indicators. It is, according to Siggel (2007, 5), an "ambiguous concept," because of a failure to rigorously define competitiveness in the early economic literature. "Competitiveness" is used interchangeably with "comparative advantage," "favorable business environment," and "productivity," for example. Furthermore, underlying structural factors that influence productivity may not show up directly in measures of competitiveness but may account for improved terms of trade.

The interest in competitiveness has increased in recent decades at the national and firm levels, as economists and academics producing the business literature once more seek to understand why some countries grow faster than others and why some firms and regions fare better than others.[1] An abundance of indicators is used to measure competitiveness at the national, regional, industry, and firm level. Indicators measure the success of countries in facilitating an economic environment that enables firms' domestic and global competitiveness. Categorizing these indicators into discrete units is difficult, given the difficulty in sometimes differentiating cause from effect; but some broad classifications are possible, for example, narrow versus broad measures, macro versus micro, short term versus long term, price versus nonprice.

The following sections identify the various elements of competitiveness and address price and nonprice measures of competitiveness.

Elements of Competitiveness

Economists from the classical school, most notably Adam Smith, equated competitiveness with the market mechanism arising from the production and distribution of goods and services based on price and quality. Thus, by this view output and wealth are created at the micro level. The nature and productivity of the economic activities taking place is paramount. Purely local industries count for competitiveness, because their productivity not only sets their wages but also has a major influence on the cost of doing business and the cost of living in the country. Competitiveness among enterprises relies on (1) efficiency, that is, being productive; (2) choice,[2] since in order to be competitive, an enterprise needs to choose those domains in which its productivity provides greater value added than that of its competitors[3]; and (3) resources, since an enterprise makes choices based upon the resources it can mobilize; included here are government, infrastructure, technology, finance, and education (Garelli 2011).

The quality of the business environment is critical for a firm's productivity. Porter's diamond theory (see for example Porter et al. 2008) explains how the business environment affects competitiveness. The diamond model (figure 2.1) incorporates (1) factor (input) conditions (natural endowments, human resources, capital availability, physical infrastructure, administrative infrastructure, information infrastructure, scientific and technological infrastructure); (2) context for firm strategy and rivalry (local rules and incentives that encourage investment and productivity, vigorous local competition); (3) related and supporting industries (capable, locally based suppliers and supporting industries, presence of clusters instead of isolated firms); and (4) demand industries (demanding and sophisticated local customers and needs).

Figure 2.1 Business Environment Quality: The Diamond

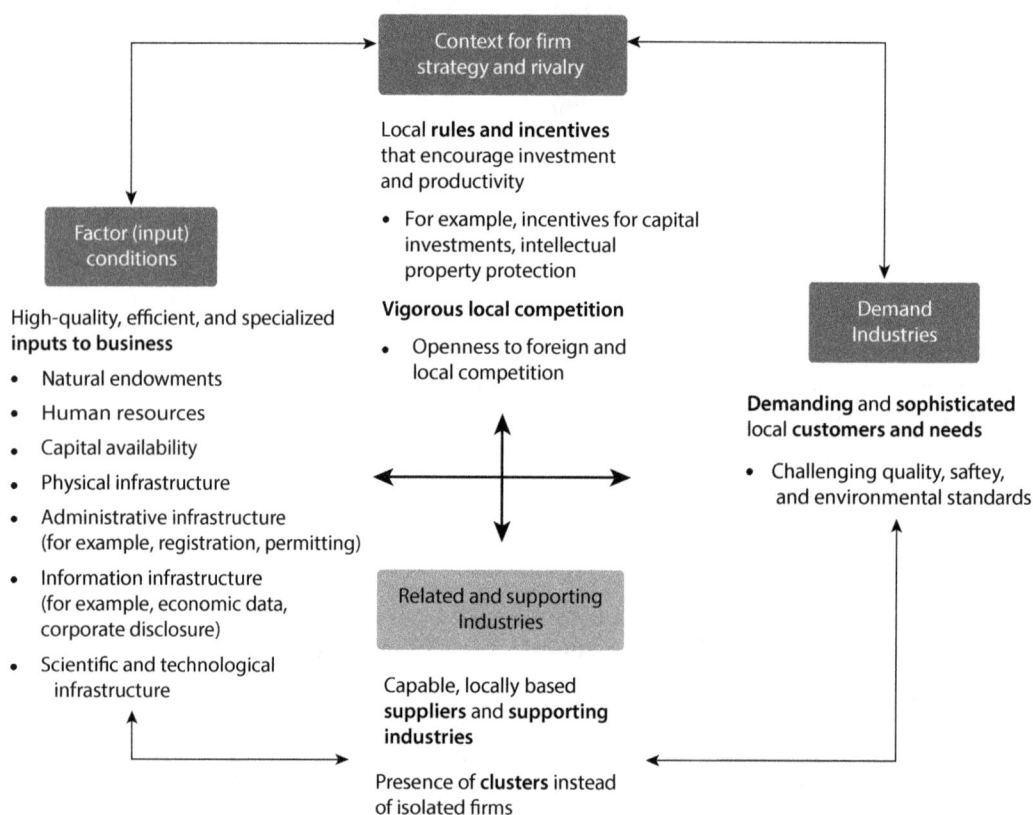

Source: Porter et al. 2008. © World Economic Forum. Used with permission; further permission required for reuse.

The success of nations is linked to prosperity that derives from economic growth plus "something else" (Garelli 2011, 489). The something else depends upon the level of development of the underlying economy—perhaps access to food and shelter in poorer countries or environmental protection in more developed economies. Unlike enterprises, nations do not generate economic value added by themselves but play a more indirect role by creating an environment that supports the activities of enterprises, including innovation. Advances in communications and globalization work increase the interdependence between nations and enterprises (Garelli 2011).

Regions and metropolises play a key role in the study of competitiveness. Globalization has made regions, port cities, and inner cities hubs of economic activity, particularly in manufacturing, commerce, and service industries. Business support services, hi-tech and biotech parks, industrial clusters, and information and communication technology (ICT) centers are all springing up to take full advantage of the agglomeration effects of concentrated economic activity and globalization. Mobile factors of production, in addition to promoting the ever-increasing movement of goods and services across geographical boundaries, are leading to rapid urbanization and bringing in their train the need for green spaces, smart spaces (research and development [R&D] firms and universities and colleges for high-skilled workers), support services, essential infrastructure, and affordable housing for the masses. Linking competitiveness to spatial development has implications for urban governance in that it improves location advantages and ensures availability of high-skilled workers, managers, and entrepreneurs.

At the global level, a country is said to be competitive if it is able to hold or increase its share of products (exports) in the world economy. Undervaluing or devaluing a nation's currency relative to other currencies to gain a competitive advantage, or using industrial policy to increase exports (through subsidies, tariffs on substitutable imports, lower wages in export industries, and/or aid-for-trade), can however bring problems of its own. The need to keep wages low or follow a two-track wage structure (one for cheap exports and a higher one for domestic consumption) reveals a lack of true competitiveness and holds down an economy's average standard of living. Similarly, government subsidies for preferred industries and sectors burden public finances, drain national income, and bias choices away from the most productive use of the nation's resources. Undervaluation and devaluation of exchange rates imply a collective national pay cut by discounting the products and services sold in world markets, while raising the cost of the goods and services imported from abroad. Therefore, in a dynamic world, the best policy is to have in place measures that continually increase productivity both at the micro level (farms and firms) and at the macro or national level.

Many exporters in developing economies face persistent barriers to competing in global markets.[4] Guilherme Reis and Farole (2012, 3) identify the barriers that arise from distortionary macroeconomic policies, poor factory conditions, and ineffective public policies that "prevent the exploitation of intra- and

Figure 2.2 The Three Pillars of Trade Competitiveness

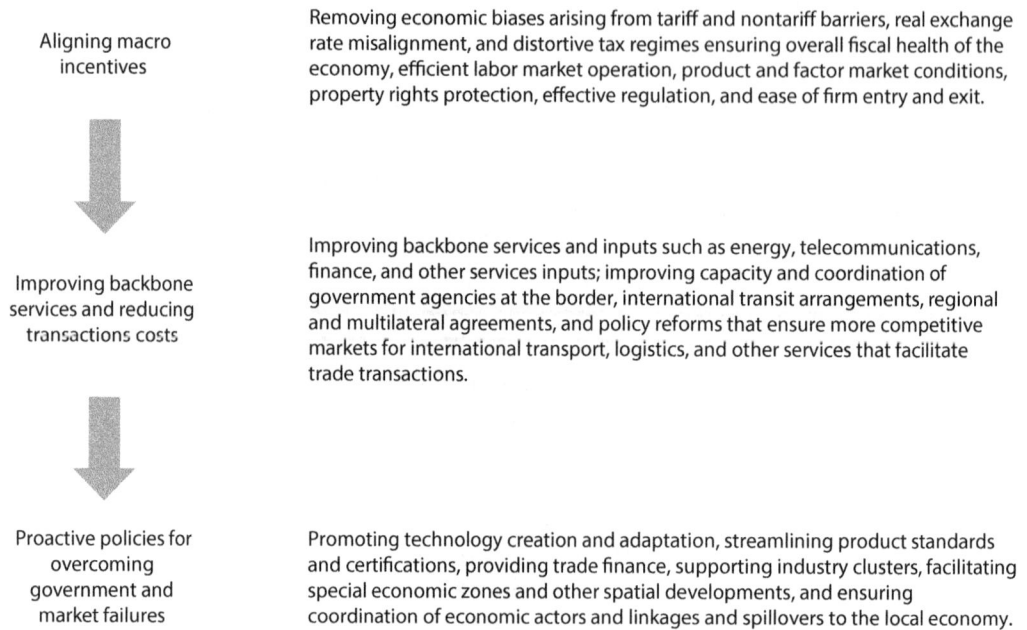

Aligning macro incentives

Removing economic biases arising from tariff and nontariff barriers, real exchange rate misalignment, and distortive tax regimes ensuring overall fiscal health of the economy, efficient labor market operation, product and factor market conditions, property rights protection, effective regulation, and ease of firm entry and exit.

Improving backbone services and reducing transactions costs

Improving backbone services and inputs such as energy, telecommunications, finance, and other services inputs; improving capacity and coordination of government agencies at the border, international transit arrangements, regional and multilateral agreements, and policy reforms that ensure more competitive markets for international transport, logistics, and other services that facilitate trade transactions.

Proactive policies for overcoming government and market failures

Promoting technology creation and adaptation, streamlining product standards and certifications, providing trade finance, supporting industry clusters, facilitating special economic zones and other spatial developments, and ensuring coordination of economic actors and linkages and spillovers to the local economy.

Source: Guilherme Reis and Farole 2012.

interindustry spillovers." The existence of these leads to what Guilherme Reis and Farole (2012, 3) refer to as "the emergence of the 'behind-the-border' or 'competitiveness' agenda, which targets the supply-side constraints to export performance." This competitiveness approach can be structured on three pillars (see figure 2.2).

Defining Competitiveness

Boltho (1996, 3) suggests that the measure of competitiveness is "relative price and/or cost indices expressed in some common currency." This definition refers to the short term and assumes by implication that structural factors do not feature. For example, price competitiveness will be said to increase in a scenario whereby outward investment rises predicated on lower government borrowing, leading to a decline in the value of the domestic currency as export prices fall and import prices increase in domestic currency terms. However, such price competitiveness is unsustainable, especially if the increase in import prices causes domestic inflation to rise, or if productivity falls in light of lower inward investment (Cantwell 2005).

On the other hand, cost-based competitiveness is more substantive in a scenario in which a fall in, for example, unit labor costs leads to lower prices, in turn causing exports to increase and imports to fall, with a resultant increase in the value of the domestic currency. In this scenario, "the perspective rise in the value of the currency is simply the reflection of competitiveness, defined as a relatively rapid growth in productivity and the value of (output and) exports" (Cantwell 2005, 547). An increasing value of the domestic currency by itself is not the achievement of competitiveness.

A broader definition of competitiveness examines the medium- and long-run effect of structural factors on economic performance. Economies are competitive when they specialize according to their factor endowments and begin to trade with one another. Krugman (1994, 30, 44) criticized the concept of "national competitiveness" that referred to an economy as more or less competitive when compared to another economy. He cautioned against the "dangerous obsession with competitiveness." Unlike enterprises, competitiveness among nations is a nonzero sum game—when nations engage in trade based on specialization arising from their factor endowments each participant benefits. In other words, countries need to build dynamic comparative advantage. Ricardo's theory of comparative advantage represents the earliest attempt to understand how nations compete.[5] Cantwell (2005, 3) suggests that at the country level, "competitiveness is about the way in which the pattern of international trade evolves over time to reflect changing capabilities and hence comparative advantage." Thus, it is more about the evolution in the comparative advantage of countries. He cites a number of authors who have contributed to the literature on this position,[6] and he examines in detail the relationship between innovation and competitiveness at the firm, industry, national, and regional level.

Lall (2001) suggests the ways in which countries can build comparative advantage, depending upon the level of government involvement. Government may provide help for market failure at a functional or a selective level where markets and institutions are deficient. On the other hand, it has no role when factor accumulation is driven solely by free markets and well-functioning institutions.

Nabi and Luthria (2002) examine the role of government in facilitating competitiveness at the company level by focusing on the demand- and supply-side determinants of competitiveness. They suggest that the role of government is more indirect when it comes to the demand-side factors, such as shareholders, competitors, bank supervisors, and creditors, but more direct when supply-side considerations—such as technology, human capital, and supply chain—are taken into account. Table 2.1 lists the determinants that they identify as important.

The definition of competitiveness that has evolved over the previous two to three decades from the business school literature reflects a multifaceted concept that includes nations as well as enterprises.[7] The Institute for Strategy and Competitiveness at Harvard University suggests that "a nation's prosperity depends on its competitiveness, which is based on the productivity with which it produces goods and services. ... Many determinants of competitiveness are regional and local, requiring economic strategies for cities and states, not just nations."

Stéphane Garelli (2011, 49), director of the World Competitiveness Center, provides an academic definition, "Competitiveness of nations is a field of economic theory, which analyzes the facts and policies that shape the ability of

Table 2.1 The Who, What, and How of Firms' Competitiveness

Who/what	Firm level	How		
		Other firms	Institutions (public-private)	International agreements
Demand-side factors Shareholders	Auditing and accounting standards, code of ethics, disclosure rules, minority shareholders' rights	n.a.	n.a.	n.a.
Competitors	Competition law and policy, antitrust laws, dealing with treatment of mergers, unilateral behavior of powerful corporations, horizontal agreements, vertical restraints, privatization, deregulation	n.a.	n.a.	n.a.
Bank supervisors	Prudential and regulatory standards, other financial institution supervision practices	n.a.	n.a.	n.a.
Creditors	Bankruptcy & secured lending regime, debtor-creditor relations, voting rules for institutional investors	n.a.	n.a.	n.a.
Supply-side factors Adapt, absorb, and modify technologies	Devote resources to R&D	Spillovers, diffusion	Measurement, standards, testing, and quality; research and technology laboratories	Intellectual property protection agreements, WTO membership
Attract, build, and retain human capital	Devote resources to in-firm training	Spillovers (hiring workers trained by other firms, joint training arrangements)	Educational institutions, skills development fund, vocational training institutes	Exchange and training agreements
Manage logistics and improve the supply chain	Devote resources to supplier and vendor development programs	Coordination among firms to integrate production and information systems	Physical infrastructure, quality, & certification institutions	Antitrust, e-commerce agreements

Source: Nabi and Luthria 2002.

Note: R&D = research and development; n.a. = not applicable; WTO = World Trade Organization.

Table 2.2 Definition of Competitiveness and Its Underlying Elements

Definition	Comments
"Competitiveness of nations is a field of Economic theory …"	This is a new field taught and researched since 1980. Its origins can be traced to the Classical Economists. Ricardo's (1819) theory of comparative advantage underlies competitiveness.
"… which analyzes facts and policies …"	Facts are endogenous, for example, an economy's natural resources and geographic location area are a given. Policies affect human effort and are affected by human effort.
"… that shape the ability of a nation to create and maintain an environment …"	Facts as outlined above and policies work to establish the competitive framework. Incorporating the word "maintain" suggests that the competitive framework should be for the long term.
"… that sustains more value creation for its enterprises …"	The emphasis on "more" suggests that nations continuously strive to fully exploit their competitiveness potential.
"… and more prosperity for its people."	This is the ultimate objective of competitiveness—to raise prosperity that may be defined as a mix of income, standard of living, and quality of life. Using the word "prosperity" allows us to emphasize the noneconomic side of competitiveness and ensure that the economic strategy of a firm, nation, or region is not competitiveness at all costs.

Source: Garelli 2011.

a nation to create and maintain an environment that sustains more value creation for its enterprises and more prosperity for its people." Table 2.2 examines the elements underlying the definition.

Porter et al. (2008, 44) suggests that "competitiveness, then, is measured by productivity" and that productivity determines the prosperity of an economy. Thus, competitiveness determines prosperity also. This interpretation relies upon a broader concept of productivity than the simple output-per-employee-per-hour construct that is most readily understood in a manufacturing context but is difficult to replicate in the services sector.

A framework for the study of competitiveness would include the outcome variable of "prosperity" that arises from the combination of "productivity" (that is, competitiveness) and "endowments." Microeconomic and macroeconomic factors determine competitiveness. Figure 2.3 summarizes the framework for the study of competitiveness.

Endowments

Endowments refer to a nation's assets—its land, people, and natural resources. A nation may be rich in assets—may have, for example, a favorable geographic location or an abundance of natural resources. Furthermore, "it could be considered that infrastructure, industrial power, and even education and skills are assets that have been accumulated by past generations" (Garelli 2011, 496). These may not necessarily be competitive, as a nation may be complacent about its endowments. It is important to differentiate between wealth and competitiveness. Studies of competitiveness should control for endowments so

Figure 2.3 Outcomes and Determinants of Competitiveness

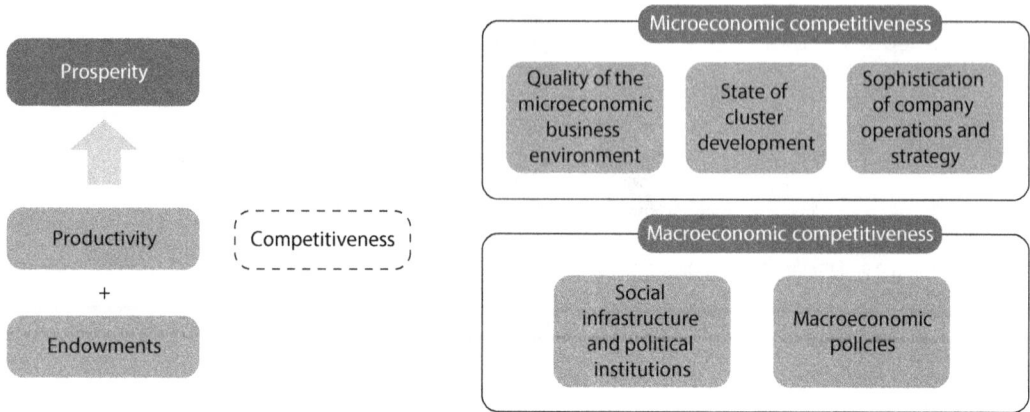

that the outcome reflects competitiveness, that is, the value added to labor and natural resources arising from productive economic activity, rather than the wealth effects arising from resource abundance. The growth literature suggests a negative effect of natural resource abundance on prosperity. This counterintuitive finding has been explained by the Dutch disease concept, whereby a nation's rising prosperity, reflected in increasing exports and an appreciation of its exchange rate, is eroded because of "factors of production moving into local activities such as retailing that have lower long-term potential for productivity growth" (Porter et al. 2008, 45).

Productivity

The broadest measure of productivity is gross domestic product (GDP) per capita. But how does this relate to competitiveness, given that this measure is arguably both a cause and effect of competitiveness? Sustainable economic growth in an economy supports competitiveness. Krugman (1994, 35) suggests that "competitiveness is a poetic way of saying productivity." Competitiveness is measured by productivity. The higher the level of productivity in an economy, the more that economy can support higher wages, positive returns to capital (both human and physical), a strong currency, and a high standard of living.

Microeconomic Competitiveness

Microeconomic factors impact directly on the productivity of firms. These factors are affected by "companies, academic institutions, and many business associations" as well as government, central and local (Porter et al. 2008, 47). Distinguishing between outcomes and determinants helps both the market and government in providing the necessary conditions to strengthen the determinants of competitiveness and facilitate the best possible outcome. Porter et al. (2008) suggests two areas of microeconomic competitiveness in this regard—company competitiveness and business environment competitiveness. A third area—cluster development—is also relevant, but data difficulties prevent it from being analyzed separately, and it is therefore considered part of the business environment.[8]

Macroeconomic Competitiveness

Macroeconomic factors also affect the productivity of firms, albeit indirectly. As noted by Porter et al. (2008, 46), "they are necessary but not sufficient for higher productivity." Fiscal policy is thought to weakly affect long-term differences in productivity across geographic areas. Spending and revenue decisions by government affect the overall prosperity of an economy and indirectly the productivity of its enterprises. Productivity is also affected by "the sustainability of government financing over time." For example, high debt levels need to be financed, with implications for spending and revenue. The effect of fiscal policy on the business cycle will also impact the productivity level of firms; "more cyclicality can increase the periods of time in which companies with financing constraints are unable to finance otherwise-profitable long-term investments" (Porter et al. 2008, 47). Monetary policy has a role to play in ensuring a stable and low rate of inflation. Volatile and high rates of inflation can put off investment decisions that might have led to higher productivity in the long run.

Social Infrastructure and Political Institutions

Social infrastructure and political institutions (SIPIs) have generated significant research attention in recent decades. Three dimensions have been identified in the Global Competitiveness Index (GCI) for summarizing SIPIs. These are basic human capacity, political institutions, and rule of law. Basic human capacity refers to basic education, health care, and a clean environment. Political institutions refer to the rules and regulations that govern the economy. Rule of law refers to the existence of property rights and the ability to protect legal rights against private and public interests (Porter et al. 2008).

In summary, the definitions of competitiveness suggest that a number of indicators are relevant for measuring this economic concept. As noted, it is an ambiguous concept, and differentiating cause from effect is critical in understanding the underlying factors of competitiveness at the national, industry, and firm level. The following sections examine a number of indicators—both price and nonprice indicators—differentiating within this broad framework those indicators from a macroeconomic perspective and those from a microeconomic perspective. See box 2.1 for a discussion of price and nonprice competitiveness in Armenia.

Price Indicators of Competitiveness

The narrowest measures of competitiveness are those indicators based on relative prices or costs. Krugman (2011) writes that "measures of relative costs and prices are, in fact, commonly—and unobjectionably—referred to as competitiveness

Box 2.1 Price and Nonprice Indicators of Competitiveness: The Case of Armenia

Weber and Yang (2011) examine competitiveness in Armenia, based on price and nonprice indicators of competitiveness. The authors note a loss in external competitiveness in Armenia from 2008, specifically its declining share of world exports (figure B2.1.1) and an appreciation in its real effective exchange rate (figure B2.1.2).

Nonprice indexes of competitiveness suggest a similar loss in competitiveness. Armenia was ranked 98 out of 139 countries in 2010 by the *Global Competitiveness Report*. Figure B2.1.3

Figure B2.1.1 Armenia's Share of World Exports

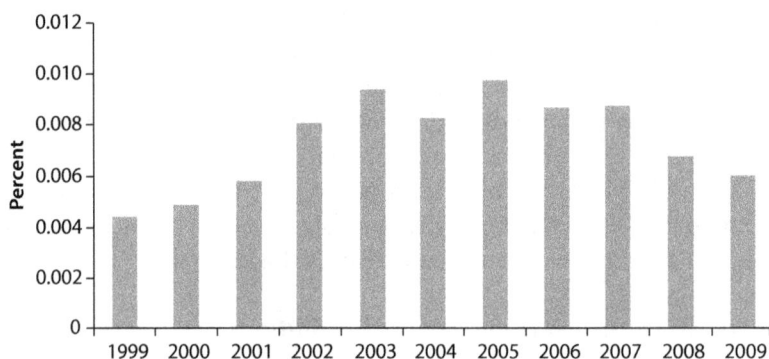

Source: Weber and Yang 2011.

Figure B2.1.2 Nominal and Real Effective Exchange Rates for Armenia

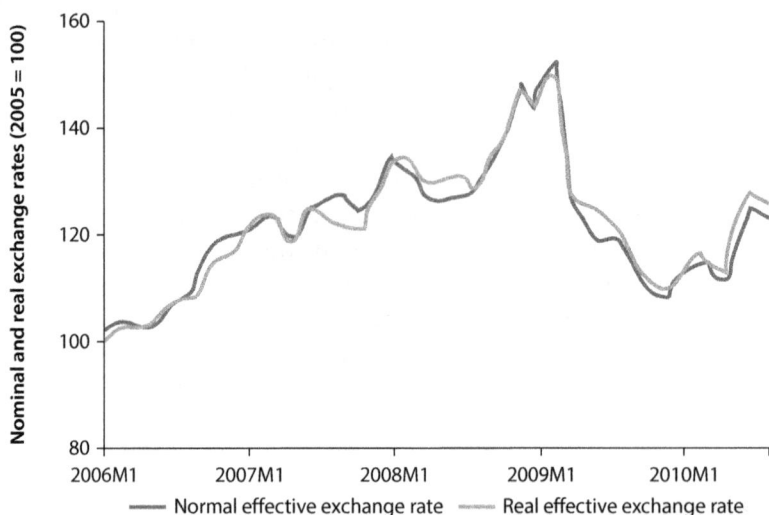

— Normal effective exchange rate   ---- Real effective exchange rate

Source: Weber and Yang 2011.
Note: M1 = month 1.

box continues next page

Box 2.1 Price and Nonprice Indicators of Competitiveness: The Case of Armenia *(continued)*

Figure B2.1.3 GDP Dynamics and Global Competitiveness Rankings for Armenia

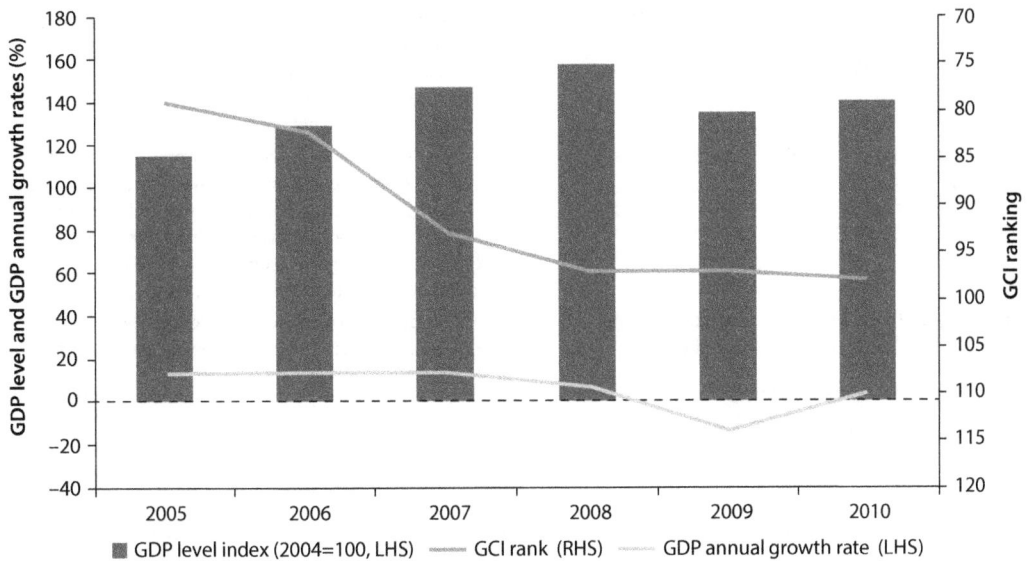

| GDP level index (2004=100, LHS) | GCI rank (RHS) | GDP annual growth rate (LHS) |

Source: Weber and Yang 2011.
Note: GDP = gross domestic product; GCI = Global Competitiveness Index.

examines gross domestic product (GDP) and global competitiveness rankings for Armenia. The strong growth record—an increase by "about 12 percent on average during 2005–08" coexisted with a declining Global Competitiveness Index (GCI) ranking (Weber and Yang 2011, 8). The poor index ranking stems primarily from the difficulties in doing business in Armenia. Respondents to the survey cite crime, corruption, theft, disorder, and difficulties in accessing finance as major impediments to doing business (Weber and Yang 2011).

indicators." The European Central Bank (ECB) publishes harmonized competitiveness indicators (HCIs) that provide measures of the euro area countries' price and cost competitiveness consistent with the real effective exchange rates (REERs) of the euro. The HCIs are available based on (1) consumer price indexes, (2) GDP deflators, and (3) unit labor cost indexes for the whole economy. Those based on consumer price indexes are the most widely used; they offer the best data quality and comparability and are timely. However, they often include goods that are not tradable and omit goods that are tradable and that are affected by indirect taxes and subsidies. Indicators based on GDP deflators may be affected by volatility in quarterly GDP figures. Similarly, unit labor costs may be affected by volatility and are subject to revision.[9]

In his study of international competitiveness, Siggel (2007) identifies those authors or institutions that use price and cost indicators of competitiveness. Table 2.3 summarizes his discussion.

Table 2.3 Price and Cost Indicators of Competitiveness

Author	Indicator	Comments
Lipschitz and McDonald (1991); Marsh and Tokarick (1994); Helleiner (1991), IMF	Real exchange rate, real effective exchange rate	Indicator(s) are associated with a macroeconomic concept of competitiveness; indicators are unidimensional in that they measure the degree of misalignment of the currency, which enhances or reduces international competitiveness. Indicator(s) can have a static or dynamic interpretation depending on how they are used.
Durand and Giorno (1987); Helleiner (1991); Jorgenson and Kuroda (1992), OECD	Price competitiveness	Price ratios are associated with a microeconomic concept of competitiveness common in microeconomic studies of single industry competitiveness where the relative industry price relative to one or more foreign competitors is translated by the exchange rate, formally resembling the real exchange rate except that prices relate to one industry only.
Hickman (1992); Turner and Golub (1997)	Unit labor costs/relative unit labor costs	Cost competitiveness is a microeconomic concept of competitiveness and is a unidimensional measure at the industry level.

Source: Siggel 2007.
Note: IMF = International Monetary Fund; OECD = Organisation for Economic Co-operation and Development.

However, the link between relative prices and costs at an international level on the one hand and a country's economic performance on the other is not always straightforward. Turner and Van't Dack (1993, 9) note that the international "relative price and cost position can be both cause and result of a country's economic performance." For example, high relative prices and costs will hamper a country's competitiveness internationally, but the levels may stem from an exchange rate appreciation. The appreciation may arise from firms in the economy competing successfully on nonprice factors such as innovation, flexibility, and high-quality goods. Increasing prices and wages suggest a worsening of competitiveness, but they are in fact a symptom of success. Also contributing to the ambiguity is the large number of measures in use for prices and costs and the divergences among these measures.

Turner and Van't Dack (1993) examine narrow measures of international competitiveness based on relative prices and costs expressed in a common currency or the REER.[10] Underlying the real effective rate is the nominal effective rate, and while this is not usually used as an indicator of competitiveness,[11] its derivation has implications for the construction of the real effective rate. Three issues are of note: the choice of the currency basket, the choice of weights, and the base period. The literature concentrates mostly on the first two issues.

The choice of weights depends upon the export-import profile of the host country. In countries where only exporters compete, global weights are used. In these situations, "the currencies of partner countries are weighted in proportion to their share in world trade" (Turner and Van't Dack 1993, 21). Bilateral weights are relevant in situations where the domestic producer is the sole competitor in each export market; that is, there is no competition from exporters from third markets. Both global and bilateral weights are special cases of the most commonly applied weights—double weights. These weights apply when "domestic producers of import substitutes face competition from the various foreign producers exporting to the domestic market" (Turner and Van't Dack 1993, 18), and when exporters to that market face competition from one another. Double weights are applied to exporting activity in which the bilateral exchange rates of a country and its competitor countries are weighted according to (1) each country's contribution to the total supply of competing goods in each separate domestic market and (2) the relative importance of each market in the given country's international trade (Turner and Van't Dack 1993). Turner and Van't Dack (1993, 18) express this formally as follows

Import weight $w_j^m = m_j^i l m_j$

Export weight $w_j^x = \left(\dfrac{x_j^i}{x_j}\right)\left(\dfrac{y_i}{y_i + \sum_h x_h^i}\right) + \sum_{k+i}\left(\dfrac{x_i^k}{x_j}\right)\left(\dfrac{x_i^k}{y_k + \sum_h x_h^k}\right)$

Overall weight $w_i = \left(\dfrac{m_j}{x_j + m_i}\right)w_i^m + \left(\dfrac{x_j}{x_j + m_j}\right)w_i^x$

where $x_j^i\left(m_j^i\right)$ = exports (imports) of country j to (from) country i

$x_j(m_j)$ = total exports (imports) of country j

y_i = domestic production in country j for its home market

The choice of currencies in the currency basket is quite narrow, given the vagaries of currencies linked to major international currencies, the fact that some currencies are nonconvertible and others are convertible at multiple exchange rates, and the fact that nominal exchange rate indexes include only those currencies from countries with stable and moderate rates of inflation. "Up to about two dozen" currencies are included in the currency basket (Turner and Van't Dack 1993, 15).

The double weight system is the most widely used. International institutions such as the International Monetary Fund (IMF), Organisation for Economic Co-operation and Development (OECD), and European Commission use this system in addition to the central bank in the United Kingdom, France, Germany, Italy, Spain, and the Netherlands (Turner and Van't Dack 1993). Quantitative differences in the derived weights are attributed to the disaggregation in trade when calculating the weights.[12] The U.S. Federal Reserve and the Bank of Canada do not use the double weight methodology but instead use the global weights index.

The REER is the nominal rate deflated by weighted measures of prices or costs. A distinction is usually made between the REER deflated by prices and that deflated by costs. In markets for homogenous goods, price competitiveness is not very relevant, for example. For differentiated goods, both price and cost matter in maintaining market share. There are a number of prices that can be used when computing the REER, each with its own advantages and disadvantages; these are discussed by Turner and Van't Dack (1993) and summarized in table 2.4.

A wide range of cost indicators has also been used in constructing the REER. However, as noted by Turner and Van't Dack (1993, 30), "cost as a notion is far from unambiguous." Labor costs are the most commonly used largely due to data availability and ease of comparison. A disadvantage is their inability to take account of productivity changes. Marsh and Tokarick (1994, 11) define an index of unit labor costs as "the ratio of an index of hourly compensation per worker in the manufacturing sector to an index of output per man hour."[13]

Marsh and Tokarick (1994) discuss five indicators of competitiveness: real exchange rates based on consumer price indexes, export unit values of manufacturing goods, the relative price of traded to nontraded goods, normalized unit labor costs in manufacturing, and the ratio of normalized unit labor costs to value-added deflators in manufacturing. Each of these is related to an economy's balance of trade in goods and nonfactor services in a way that has implications for that country's competitiveness. Their conclusion is that no one indicator is

Table 2.4 Price Measures of Competitiveness

Price index	Advantages	Disadvantages	Use
Relative export prices	Obvious choice for gauging price competitiveness in market conditions where some degree of pricing independence exists	Force of international competition will limit observed differences in export prices Calculation is limited to goods actually traded—ignores goods that are potentially traded Indexes used for prices are derived from unit value indexes based on average value of goods traded and can be heavily influenced by composition of exports Timeliness of data—measured export unit values relate to prices set in past Use of export prices alone is inconsistent with double weighting scheme, especially where domestic producer prices are more relevant for domestically produced and sold goods	Most international institutions produce real effective exchange rates calculated on this basis
Consumer prices	Calculated on basis of a basket of goods that is fairly comparable across countries Data are readily available and timely	May be poor proxies of tradable goods Consumer prices include goods and services that are not traded Excludes capital goods Affected by indirect taxes, subsidies, and price controls As final goods prices, they do not take into account (traded) intermediate goods	Widely used
Wholesale prices or industrial producer prices	Sometimes chosen to approximate more closely prices of tradable goods Prices reflect primarily in the more active industrial sector	Prices are based on turnover and tend to overweight raw commodities and semi-manufactured goods Sometimes high weight given to imported goods makes the index unsuitable for evaluating the competitiveness of domestic production	IMF

Source: Turner and Van't Dack 1993.
Note: IMF = International Monetary Fund.

a true representation of an economy's competitiveness. The authors suggest "competitiveness indicators should be used in conjunction with other indicators in order to obtain an assessment of competitiveness that is as complete as possible" (Marsh and Tokarick 1994, iii).

Nonprice Indicators of Competitiveness

Three international annual publications in particular shed light on nonprice competitiveness. These are the *World Competitiveness Yearbook* (WCY) published by the International Institute for Management Development (IMD 2012), the *Global Competitiveness Report* published by the World Economic Forum (WEF 2009, 2012), and the *Doing Business* report published by the World Bank Group (2012). The reports include readily measurable indicators of competitiveness as well as indicators that are more qualitative in nature and rely upon survey responses. Survey responses can capture those indicators that are less amenable to quantification, such as an economy's capacity for technological innovation, its degree of product specialization, and the quality of the products and after-sales service, and also those factors that contribute indirectly to improved competitiveness. The following sections examine the indicators of competitiveness from these three publications.

The WCY

The IMD has published competitiveness rankings for selected OECD countries and newly industrialized countries since 1989 in its annual publication, the WCY. The IMD website explains that "the WCY ranks and analyzes the ability of nations to create and maintain an environment in which enterprises can compete."[14] Since 2001, the WCY has relied on the country scores achieved on four factors, which rely themselves on five subfactors related to the national environment (for competitiveness).[15] See table 2.5.

The 20 subfactors comprise more than 300 criteria—331 in 2011. Each subfactor has a different number of criteria, although each subfactor has the same weight in the overall calculation of results. Two-thirds of the criteria are "hard data," that is, they make use of data that can be measured, such as GDP. The remaining one-third comprises survey data. Aggregating the 20 subfactors yields the competitiveness score for each country in the sample.

Table 2.5 Factors and Subfactors Comprising the National Environment (World Competitiveness Yearbook)

Economic performance	Government efficiency	Business efficiency	Infrastructure
Domestic economy	Public finance	Productivity	Basic infrastructure
International trade	Fiscal policy	Labor market	Technological infrastructure
International investment	Institutional framework	Finance	Scientific infrastructure
Employment	Business legislation	Management practices	Health and environment
Prices	Societal framework	Attitudes and values	Education

Source: IMD, "Research Methodology," http://www.imd.org/research/centers/wcc/research_methodology.cfm.

The Global Competitiveness Report

The goal of the *Global Competitiveness Report*, published by the WEF, is to "provide insight and stimulate discussion among all stakeholders on the best strategies and policies to overcome the obstacles to improved competitiveness." The WEF uses the GCI, "a comprehensive tool that measures the microeconomic and macroeconomic foundations of national competitiveness," for its analysis (WEF 2012, 4).[16] The index represents a weighted average of variables that are grouped into 12 "pillars" of competitiveness and that summarize a set of institutions, policies, and factors that determine the productivity level of an economy. The weights assigned depend upon the level of development of the economy. The WEF identifies three types of development and categorizes countries as possessing basic requirements, efficiency enhancers, or innovation and sophistication factors (table 2.6).

The 12 identified pillars may be grouped according to an economy's stage of development—that is, some pillars are more relevant for specific stages of development (see figure 2.4).

At the *basic requirements* stage of development, an economy is likely to be factor driven, with large pools of unskilled labor. Its sources of competitiveness stem from its factor endowments. Competition is based on price, and low productivity is reflected in low wages. Maintaining competitiveness relies on well-functioning public and private institutions, a stable macroeconomic environment, and a healthy population with at least a basic education.

Institutions (pillar 1) represent the legal and administrative framework of an economy within which individuals, firms, and government interact for the people's welfare. Institutions are also influenced by the attitude of government toward markets and the manner in which government conducts its own operations. Bureaucracy, red tape, corruption, and lack of transparency impose large costs on businesses and hinder economic growth and development. The recent global crisis has revealed the importance of private

Table 2.6 Subindex Weights and Income Thresholds for Stages of Development (Global Competitiveness Index)

	Stage 1: factor driven	Transition from stage 1 to state 2	Stage 2: efficiency driven	Transition from stage 2 to stage 3	Stage 3: innovation driven
GDP per capita (US$) thresholds[a]	< 2,000	2,000–2,999	3,000–8,999	9,000–17,000	> 17,000
Weight for basic requirements subindex (%)	60	40–60	40	20–40	20
Weight for efficiency enhancers subindex (%)	35	35–50	50	50	50
Weight for innovation and sophistication factors subindex (%)	5	5–10	10	10–30	30

Source: WEF 2012.

Notes: GDP = gross domestic product.

a. For economies with a high dependency on mineral resources, GDP per capita is not the sole criterion for the determination of the stage of development.

Figure 2.4 The 12 Pillars of Competitiveness

Pillar	Basic requirements		
1	Institutions		
2	Infrastructure	→	Key for factor-driven economies
3	Macroeconomic environment		
4	Health and primary education		
	Efficiency enhancers		
5	Higher education and training		
6	Goods market efficiency		
7	Labor market efficiency	→	Key for efficiency-driven economies
8	Financial market development		
9	Technological readiness		
10	Market size		
	Innovation and sophistication factors		Key for innovation-driven economies
11	Business sophistication	→	
12	Innovation		

Source: WEF 2012. © World Economic Forum. Used with permission; further permission required for reuse.

institutions, including accounting standards, transparency, and mutual trust in competitiveness. The quality of institutions impacts on competitiveness and growth because it influences key investment decisions by one and all in the economy. The quality of the institutional framework is important for investment and for how efficiently an economy distributes its wealth. Good governance across private and public institutions is critical in maintaining competitiveness.

Infrastructure (pillar 2) includes transport, telecommunications, and energy. An efficient and well-functioning infrastructure is critical for growth and development. Well-developed infrastructure reduces the distance between various regions and lowers the costs of operation for everyone. In addition to enabling entrepreneurs to distribute their goods and services on time, moving workers to jobs, and enhancing growth, it helps lower nonincome poverty and reduces regional disparities.

A stable macroeconomic environment (pillar 3) is critical for economic growth and development and a necessary albeit not a sufficient condition for competitiveness. Public finance management is a major component of macroeconomic stability and an issue of particular relevance in the wake of the 2008 global financial crisis. Many of the advanced economies now face high levels of indebtedness that may have adverse consequences for competitiveness. For example:

- Sovereign debt in advanced economies may trigger a global recession in the short run.
- Higher debt levels are generally associated with higher interest rates; these create a business environment in which it is difficult to raise finance, thus lowering investment.
- Governments come under pressure to raise taxes to service debt; these taxes may be distortive or stifle further business activity.

In the long run, the impact of public debt depends on how the debt is spent—it will benefit competitiveness if it is used to finance investments that raise productivity, but if it is used to finance consumption, it will burden the economy in the long run, resulting in higher interest payments and debt service payments that take up a larger proportion of the government budget, thus forcing a reduction in spending in other areas.

A healthy population with at least a basic education (pillar 4) is vital to a country's competitiveness and productivity, and malnutrition among children does not create a healthy workforce down the road. Weak and ill workers will be less productive, and the poor health of citizens increases the costs of health care and thus doing business. Public and private investment in preventive health care and provision of health services is important. Quantity and quality of basic schooling is also an important factor for ensuring healthy practices across generations and for providing the initial building blocks upon which further advancement can take place. Without these, firms will find it difficult "to move up the value chain by producing more sophisticated or value-intensive products" (WEF 2012, 5).

As economies develop and become more competitive (reflected, for example, in increasing productivity and rising wages), they will transition to the *efficiency-driven* stage of development (figure 2.4). Economies in this stage must "begin to develop more efficient production processes and increase product quality because wages have risen and they cannot increase prices" (WEF 2012, 9). The pillars necessary for continuing competitiveness are higher education and training, efficient goods markets, well-functioning labor markets, developed financial markets, the ability to harness the benefits of existing technologies, and a large domestic or foreign market (that is, substantial market size).

Higher education and training (pillar 5) are critical for economies that would like to move up the value chain and compete in a globalized world. Highly educated workers are better able to adapt to changing production systems and meet new opportunities that the globalized work environment presents. Higher education is measured by enrollment in secondary and tertiary education and includes qualitative measures of education from evaluations by the business community. Vocational training and on-the-job training are used to measure training.

Economies with efficient goods markets (pillar 6) benefit from the right mix of products and services based on their particular supply and demand conditions.

Factors that adversely impact those conditions and stymie competitiveness are a lack of healthy market competition, perhaps due to obstructions by government intervention[17]; protectionism; and insufficient knowledge, so that (for example) sellers may fail to respond to customers' orientation or level of sophistication.

Well-functioning labor markets (pillar 7) suggest that workers are performing their jobs to their best ability and are suited to their jobs. Efficient and flexible labor markets require that workers be able to move easily between jobs, at low cost, and without social disruption owing to wage changes. From the worker's perspective, well-functioning labor markets ensure a link between worker incentives and meritocracy, and equity concerns are reflected in equal opportunities for men and women.

A well-functioning, efficient financial sector (pillar 8) ensures that savings by residents and nonresidents are put to their most effective and productive use. A properly regulated, sophisticated financial system offering financial products is imperative for business investment that leads to increased productivity in the economy.

The technological-readiness pillar (pillar 9) measures how readily an economy can adopt existing technology to increase industry productivity. Of particular importance is an economy's capacity to harness ICT. "ICT access and usage are key enablers" (WEF 2012, 7). Foreign direct investment can also play an important role in introducing new technology and best practice to the host economy.

Market size (pillar 10) is important because the larger the size of the market, the more opportunity for firms to exploit economies of scale. Globalization has extended the market to include the international market, and a large body of empirical evidence suggests a positive relationship between openness to trade and economic growth.

The third stage of development is the *innovation and sophistication factors* stage. Future progress on productivity will rely upon the production of new and different goods. Firms must be technologically efficient and engaged in expanding the economy's frontiers of technology and knowledge by innovating. Business sophistication and innovation are critical pillars in this stage. Business sophistication (pillar 11) refers to the quality of the overall business networks within a country and the quality of the individual firms' operation and strategies. The former relies upon a sufficient number of high-quality suppliers; where these are in geographic proximity to the firm, forming a cluster, productivity is heightened. "Branding, marketing, distribution, advanced production processes, and the production of unique and sophisticated products" are responsible for the firm's business sophistication (WEF 2012, 8). Technological innovation (pillar 12) "is the final pillar of competitiveness" identified by the *Global Competitiveness Report*. This pillar aims to move the economy further toward its technological and knowledge frontier by technologically efficient firms engaged in innovation. The environment for this relies upon "public and private investment, particularly in research and development (R&D); the presence of high-quality scientific research institutions; extensive collaboration in research between university and industry; and the protection of intellectual property" (WEF 2012, 8).

As noted in the *Global Competitiveness Report*, the pillars of competitiveness are strongly interrelated; for example, "a strong innovation capacity (pillar 12) will be very difficult to achieve without a healthy, well-educated and trained workforce (pillars 4 and 5) that is adept at absorbing new technologies (pillar 9), and without sufficient financing (pillar 8) for R&D or an efficient goods market that makes it possible to take new innovations to market (pillar 6)" (WEF 2012, 8). The pillars are aggregated into a single index based on weights, and results for each pillar are also published. These results provide information for an economy on gaps in competitiveness.

Doing Business: Measuring Business Regulations

The *Doing Business* project was launched in 2002 by the World Bank to look at the regulations facing small- and medium-size businesses throughout their life cycle. Quantitative data measuring business regulation environments across countries are gathered and analyzed in an annual report. The first annual report was published in 2003 and covered 5 indicator sets and 133 economies. According to the *Doing Business* website, the goal of the report is to "provide an objective basis for understanding and improving the regulatory environment for business around the world."[18] The most recent report (World Bank 2012) covers 11 indicator sets and 183 economies (see table 2.7).

The data come from two sources—one from the domestic laws and regulations and administrative requirements pertaining to businesses in the host country and the second from "time-and-motion indicators that measure the efficiency in achieving a regulatory goal (such as granting the legal identity of a business)" (World Bank 2012, 17). Most of the cost indicators are based on official fee schedules where available. For indicators such as dealing with construction permits, enforcing contracts, and resolving insolvency, the time and cost components are based on actual practice. However, the respondents are those who are very familiar with these elements of the regulatory environment—such as the professionals or government officials who routinely administer or advise on

Table 2.7 Eleven Areas of Business Regulation Measured by Doing Business

Start-up	Expansion	Operations	Insolvency
Starting a business Minimum capital requirement Procedures, time, and cost	**Registering property** Procedures, time, and cost	**Dealing with construction permits** Procedures, time, and cost	**Resolving insolvency** Time, cost, and recovery rate
	Getting credit Credit information systems Movable collateral laws	**Getting electricity** Procedures, times, and cost	
	Protecting investors Disclosure and liability in related-party transactions	**Paying taxes** Payments, time, and total tax rate	
	Enforcing contracts Procedures, time, and cost to resolve a commercial dispute	**Trading across borders** Documents, time, and cost Employing workers	

Source: World Bank 2012.

the legal and regulatory requirements covered in each topic.[19] "The credit information survey is answered by officials of the credit registry. Freight forwarders, accountants, architects, and other professionals answer the survey related to trading across borders, taxes, and construction permits" (World Bank 2012, 22). A simple averaging is applied to all topics and the components within each topic: each is weighted equally.

The indicators are based on standardized case studies where the business is located in the largest city. This approach may prove limiting in some countries where there are differences in regulations. *Doing Business* also publishes subnational studies for a range of countries and recently published a pilot study on the business environment in the second-largest city in three large economies in order to examine the within-country variations. The standardized case approach assumes a limited liability company or its equivalent.

The results from the *Doing Business* survey correlate nicely with those from other studies examining competitiveness, such as the OECD product market regulation indicators and the GCI (see figures 2.5 and 2.6).

The OECD product market regulations inform on the extent to which the regulatory environment promotes or curtails competition. They include measures on "the extent of price controls, the licensing and permit system, the degree of simplification of rules and procedures, the administrative burdens and legal and regulatory barriers, the prevalence of discriminatory procedures and the degree of government control over business enterprises" (World Bank 2012, 18). The correlation between these measures and those on the ease of doing business is .72. Furthermore, the correlation between the ease of doing business and the GCI is .82 (figure 2.6).

Figure 2.5 Correlation between Doing Business Rankings and OECD Rankings of Product Market Regulation

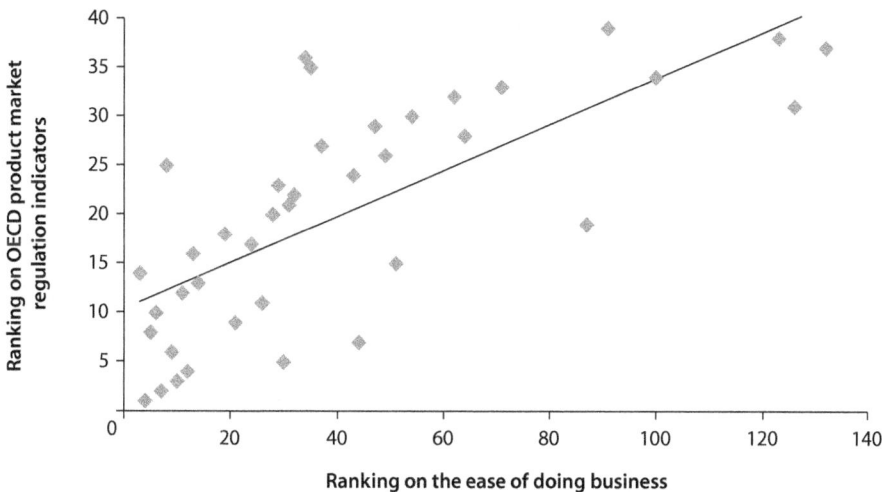

Source: World Bank 2012.
Note: OECD = Organisation for Co-operation and Development.

Figure 2.6 Correlation between Doing Business Rankings and World Economic Forum Rankings on Global Competitiveness

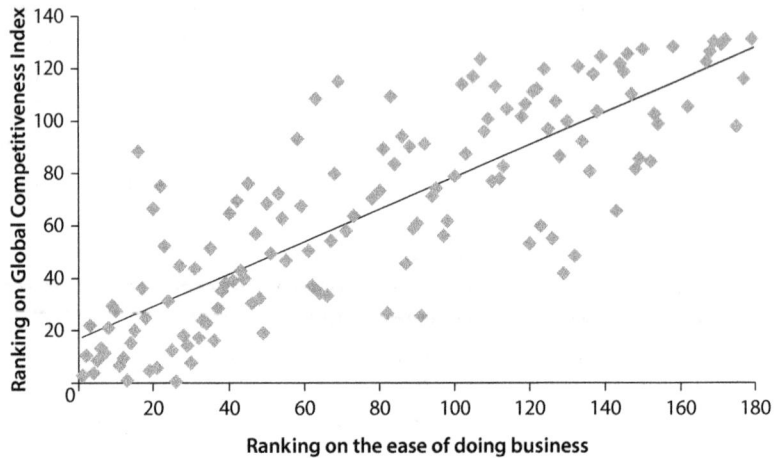

Source: World Bank 2012.

Conclusion

The chapter examined the concept of competitiveness by first noting its many applications—to the firm, the industry, the region, the nation, and the global economy. It highlighted its growing popularity among policy makers, lawmakers, and researchers. Competitiveness has been given a new impetus in the wake of the most recent financial crisis, in 2008. Stronger competitiveness is particularly relevant in a growth-challenged world.

Price and nonprice measures of competitiveness help to classify broadly the concept. Price and cost measures were identified and their advantages and disadvantages discussed. Nonprice measures have proliferated in the business literature, and annual surveys of competitiveness at the national level have become popular over the last few decades. The role of government in promoting competitiveness was referenced throughout the chapter; it is a theme that recurs throughout this book.

Notes

1. A substantial new literature has emerged from the business studies discipline.

2. Environmentally friendly choices need not be at the cost of economic competitiveness. The firm that addresses environmental improvements through innovation and new technology may actually increase its economic competitiveness. For a list of papers that examine the issue of environmental quality and competitiveness, see Institute for Strategy and Competitiveness, "Environmental Quality and Competitiveness," http://www.isc.hbs.edu/soci-environmental.htm.

3. The theory of comparative advantage (Ricardo 1819) applies this approach at the level of the economy.

4. In recognition of this, the World Bank has developed the *Trade Competitiveness Diagnostic* (TCD) toolkit. The TCD provides "a framework, guidelines, and practical tools needed to conduct an analysis of trade competitiveness. The toolkit can be used to assess the competitiveness of a country's overall basket of exports, as well as specific traded sectors" and is intended "for policy makers and practitioners involved in analysis of trade performance and design of trade and industrial policy" (Guilherme Reis and Farole 2012, 1).

5. Dwyer and Kim (2003) identify the following authors addressing the comparative advantage and/or price competitiveness aspect of competitiveness: Bellak and Weiss (1993); Cartwright (1993); Durand and Giorno (1987); Fagerberg (1988); Fakiolas (1985); Hilke and Nelson (1988); Hodgetts (1993); Porter (1990); Rugman (1991); and Rugman and D'Cruz (1993).

6. Cantwell (2005, 3) writes, "Dynamic accounts of the paths of international trade and investment were revived . . . by the technology gap approach (Posner 1961) and the product cycle model (Vernon 1966). It was only in the 1980s that scholars based at Sussex once again wedded an analysis of structural shifts over time in the pattern of international trade to a more realistic approach to innovation—see Soete 1981; Dosi and Soete 1988; Dosi, Pavitt, and Soete 1990; and Fagerberg's 1987 paper on structural changes in international trade (reprinted as chapter 7 in Fagerberg 2002)."

7. The World Economic Forum (WEF) defines competitiveness as "the set of institutions, policies and factors that determine the level of productivity of a city or region" (2007).

8. Chapter 5 in this book examines clusters and competitiveness.

9. See European Central Bank, "Harmonised Competitiveness Indicators," http://www.ecb.int/stats/exchange/hci/html/index.en.html.

10. The real effective exchange rate is the nominal rate (a weighted average of various bilateral exchange rates, with the choice and weights of the bilateral rates reflecting their relative importance to the economic issue being analyzed) deflated by a similarly weighted average of foreign prices or costs, relative to those at home (Turner and Van't Dack 1993).

11. Turner and Van't Dack (1993, 13) note that authors such as Rosensweig (1987) advocate the use of the nominal effective exchange rate as a measure of competitiveness given "its timeliness, its greater frequency, the ease of data collection and of cross-country comparability, and the avoidance of measurement errors in the price or cost series."

12. Turner and Van't Dack (1993) note that the International Monetary Fund (IMF) uses highly disaggregated manufacturing data when applying the methodology, while the European Commission includes all traded goods and services.

13. "A real exchange rate indicator is then computed by dividing the index of unit labor costs in the home country by the index of unit labor costs for the sixteen industrial countries for which data are collected by the IMF" (Marsh and Tokarick 1994, 11).

14. See http://www.imd.org/research/centers/wcc/research_methodology.cfm.

15. Up to 2001, the *World Competitiveness Yearbook* published a competitiveness score for its sample of countries based upon eight factors that comprised a number of subfactors each. The eight factors were domestic economy, internationalization, government, finance, infrastructure, management, science and technology, and people.

16. "The first version of the Global Competitiveness Index was published in 2004" (WEF 2012, 44).

17. Examples include "distortionary or burdensome taxes" and "restrictive and discriminatory rules on foreign direct investment that limit foreign ownership" (WEF 2012, 7).

18. See http://www.doingbusiness.org/about-us.

19. Estimates are made by "practitioners with significant and routine experience in the transaction" (World Bank 2012, 22).

References

Bellak, C. J., and A. Weiss. 1993. "A Note on the Austrian 'Diamond.'" *Management International Review* 33 (2): 109–18.

Boltho, A. 1996. "The Assessment: International Competitiveness." *Oxford Review of Economic Policy* 12 (3): 1–16.

Cantwell, J. 2005. "Innovation and Competitiveness." In *Handbook of Innovation*, edited by J. Fagerberg, D. C. Mowery, and R. R. Nelson, 543–67. Oxford, UK: Oxford University Press.

Cartwright, W. R. 1993. "Multiple Linked 'Diamonds' and the International Competitiveness of Export-Dependent Industries: The New Zealand Experience." *Management International Review* 33: 55–70.

Dosi, G., K. L. R. Pavitt, and L. L. G. Soete. 1990. *The Economics of Technical Change and International Trade.* London: Harvester Wheatsheaf.

Dosi, G., and L. L. G. Soete. 1988. "Technical Change and International Trade." In *Technical Change and Economic Theory*, edited by G. Dosi, C. Freeman, R. Nelson, G. Silverberg, and L. L. G. Soete, 401–30. London: Frances Pinter.

Durand, M., and C. Giorno. 1987. "Indicators of International Competitiveness: Conceptual Aspects and Evaluation." *OECD Economic Studies* 9: 147–82.

Dwyer, L., and C. Kim. 2003. "Destination Competitiveness: Determinants and Indicators." *Current Issues in Tourism* 6 (5): 369–414.

Fagerberg, J. 1988. "International Competitiveness." *Economic Journal* 98: 355–74.

———. 2002. *Technology, Growth and Competitiveness: Selected Essays.* Cheltenham, UK: Edward Elgar.

Fakiolas, T. 1985. "Basic Causes of Soviet Industry's Low International Competitiveness." *Journal of Economic Studies* 12 (5): 39–52.

Garelli, S. 2011. "The Fundamentals and History of Competitiveness." In *IMD World Competitiveness Yearbook 2011*, appendix 3. Lausanne, Switzerland: International Institute for Management Development.

Guilherme Reis, J., and T. Farole. 2012. *Trade Competitiveness Diagnostic Toolkit.* Washington, DC: World Bank.

Helleiner, G. K. 1989. "Transnational Corporations and Direct Foreign Investment." In *Handbook of Development Economics*, vol. 2, chapter 27. Amsterdam: Elsevier Science Publishers BV.

———. 1991. "Increasing International Competitiveness: A Conceptual Framework." In *Increasing the International Competitiveness of Exports from Caribbean Countries*, edited by Y. Wen and J. Sengupta, 17–26. Washington, DC: World Bank.

Hickman, B. G. 1992. "International Productivity and Competitiveness: An Overview." In *International Productivity and Competitiveness*, edited by B. G. Hickman, 3–32. New York: Oxford University Press.

Hilke, J., and P. Nelson. 1988. *US International Competitiveness: Evolution or Revolution?* New York: Praeger.

Hodgetts, R. M. 1993. "Porter's Diamond Framework in a Mexican Context." *Management International Review* 33 (special issue): 41–54.

IMD (International Institute for Management Development). 2012. *IMD World Competitiveness Yearbook 2012.* Lausanne, Switzerland: IMD.

Jorgenson, D. W., and M. Kuroda. 1992. "Productivity and International Competitiveness in Japan and the United States, 1960–1985." In *International Productivity and Competitiveness,* edited by B. G. Hickman, 203–29. New York: Oxford University Press.

Krugman, P. 1994. "Competitiveness—A Dangerous Obsession." *Foreign Affairs* 73 (2): 28–44. http://www.pkarchive.org/global/pop.html.

———. 2011. "Competitiveness." *The Conscience of a Liberal* (blog), January 22. http://krugman.blogs.nytimes.com/2011/01/22/competitiveness.

Lall, S. 2001. "Competitiveness Indices and Developing Countries: An Economic Evaluation of the Global Competitiveness Report." *World Development* 29 (9): 1501–25.

Lipschitz, L., and D. McDonald. 1991. "Real Exchange Rates and Competitiveness: A Clarification of Concepts and Some Measurements for Europe." IMF Working Paper 91/25, International Monetary Fund, Washington, DC.

Marsh, L. W., and S. P. Tokarick. 1994. "Competitiveness Indicators: A Theoretical and Empirical Assessment." Working Paper 94/29, International Monetary Fund, Washington, DC.

Nabi, I., and M. Luthria. 2002. *Building Competitive Firms: Incentives and Capabilities.* Washington, DC: World Bank.

Porter, M. E. 1990. *The Competitive Advantage of Nations.* New York: Free Press.

Porter, M. E., M. Delgado, C. Ketels, and S. Stern. 2008. "Moving to a New Global Competitiveness Index." In *The Global Competitiveness Report 2008–2009,* 43–63. World Economic Forum, Geneva, Switzerland.

Posner, M. V. 1961. "International Trade and Technical Change." *Oxford Economic Papers* 13 (3): 323–41.

Ricardo, David. 1819. *On the Principles of Political Economy and Taxation.* London, UK: John Murray.

Rosensweig, J. A. 1987. "Constructing and Using Exchange Rate Indexes." *Economic Review* (Summer): 4–16.

Rugman, A. M. 1991. "Diamond in the Rough." *Business Quarterly* 55 (3): 61–64.

Rugman, A. M., and J. R. D'Cruz. 1993. "The 'Double Diamond' Model of International Competitiveness: The Canadian Experience." *Management International Review* 33 (special issue): 17–39.

Siggel, E. 2007. "International Competitiveness and Comparative Advantage: A Survey and a Proposal for Measurement." Paper prepared for CESifo Venice Summer Institute, Venice International University, Italy, July 20–21.

Soete, L. L. G. 1981. "A General Test of Technological Gap Trade Theory." *Weltwirtschaftliches Archiv* 117 (4): 638–60.

Turner, A., and S. Golub. 1997. "Towards a System of Unit Labor Cost-Based Competitiveness Indicators for Advanced, Developing and Transition Countries." *Staff Studies for the World Economic Outlook,* 47–60. Washington, DC: International Monetary Fund.

Turner, P., and J. Van't Dack. 1993. "Measuring International Price and Cost Competitiveness." Economic Papers No. 39, Bank for International Settlements, Geneva, Switzerland.

Vernon, R. 1966. "International Investment and International Trade in the Product Cycle." *Quarterly Journal of Economics* 80 (2): 190–207.

Weber, A., and C. Yang. 2011. "Armenia: An Assessment of the Real Exchange Rate and Competitiveness." Working Paper WP/11/20, International Monetary Fund, Washington, DC.

WEF (World Economic Forum). 2009. *The Global Competitiveness Report 2008–2009.* Geneva: World Economic Forum.

———. 2010. *The Global Competitiveness Report 2010–2011.* Geneva: World Economic Forum.

———. 2012. *The Global Competitiveness Report 2012–2013.* Geneva: World Economic Forum.

World Bank. 2012. *Doing Business 2012: Doing Business in a More Transparent World.* Washington, DC: World Bank.

CHAPTER 3

National Competitiveness

Paul Krugman (1994) criticized the concept of national competitiveness nearly 20 years ago when he attested that the term was meaningless as applied to national economies. He was reacting to the view, increasingly propounded by governments and academics, that nations were in competition with one another and that only the most competitive would succeed. Indeed, he cautioned about the dangerous obsession with competitiveness applied to national economies.

Elsewhere indexes of national competitiveness were being developed to describe international competitive performance.[1] The best known of these is the Global Competitiveness Index (GCI) maintained by the World Economic Forum (WEF). The WEF defines national competitiveness as "the set of institutions, policies, and factors that determine the level of productivity of a country" (WEF 2009, 3). Competitiveness at the national level is both a static and a dynamic concept. On the one hand, productivity determines the prosperity of a nation, a prosperity that will be shared among its citizens. On the other hand, productivity also determines the returns on investment in an economy, which in turn determine the growth rate of that economy. Globalization, liberalization, and rapid technical change have contributed to the enormous emphasis on national competitiveness.

The following sections examine what is meant by national competitiveness and explore the policy implications of increasing a nation's competitiveness domestically and internationally. We present global competitiveness rankings as summarized by the International Institute for Management Development (IMD), the GCI from the WEF, and the *Doing Business* report from the World Bank.

Defining National Competitiveness

National competitiveness may be defined as "a field of economic theory, which analyzes the facts and policies that shape the ability of a nation to create and maintain an environment that sustains more value creation for its enterprises and more prosperity for its people" (Garelli 2011, 49). This definition informs the competitiveness measures developed by the WEF and the IMD. The definition provides for a broad measure of competitiveness, incorporating macroeconomic and microeconomic factors, and is discussed more fully below in the context of the country competitiveness rankings produced annually by the WEF and IMD.

In addition, other more narrow price- and cost-based measures of competitiveness are widely used to measure national competitiveness. These various measures incorporate elements such as labor productivity, consumer prices, unit labor costs, terms of trade, and Balassa's index of revealed comparative advantage, with the consumer price index (CPI)–based real effective exchange rate (REER) the most widely used measure (Bakardzhieva, Ben Naceur, and Kamar 2010).[2] The CPI-based REER takes account of price/inflation differences between trading partners after allowing for nominal effective exchange rate movements and after weighting individual country components according to trade or other such weights. Basically, in the literature, "movements in REERs provide an indication of the evolution of a country's aggregate external price competitiveness."[3] All other things held constant, an appreciation in the REER means a loss in competitiveness for the country, while a depreciation means the opposite.

However, all other things are rarely constant, and an appreciation may not always indicate a loss of competitiveness. For example, the Balassa-Samuelson effect suggests that countries with higher productivity growth in the traded goods sector experience higher prices in the nontraded goods sector and thus an appreciation in the REER as the underlying equilibrium exchange rate rises. (This effect, which is transmitted through wage movements in the nontraded sector, does not imply declining competitiveness, as higher prices reflect higher underlying productivity. For instance, although price levels are higher in, say, Germany, than in most developing countries, this does not mean that Germany is less competitive, as it is more productive.) Of interest in measuring true competitiveness gains or losses, therefore, is the distance that the REER moves from its equilibrium value, which itself changes over time for various reasons (including not only productivity movements but also terms of trade changes, the accumulation of assets, and so on).

Bearing these caveats in mind, we take a quick look, in figure 3.1, at movements in measured REER competitiveness across a set of wealthy, highly productive countries. Taking 2000 as the starting point, we can see that, all other things equal, there have been major changes in the REER over a short period (just over a decade). Among this sample, Switzerland has seen the greatest appreciation in its REER (that is, the greatest measured loss of competitiveness), while Japan has seen the largest REER depreciation (that is, the greatest measured gain in competitiveness). Of course, not all is equal, and Switzerland's equilibrium real exchange rate has likely become stronger over this period given its major accumulation of international reserves, while Japan's has probably become weaker, as its public debt position has worsened, growth has stagnated, and its external position has worsened. Another major issue is that in any chosen base year, not all countries are equal in terms of starting competitiveness. So REER measures are good at capturing changes in competitiveness rather than competitiveness levels themselves. (The WEF and IMD measures do aim to capture competitiveness levels.) Nevertheless, despite the caveats, REERs are good summary measures of competitiveness moves and are therefore widely used by policy makers and economists alike.

Figure 3.1 REER Competitiveness Gains and Losses, Selected Countries, 2000–11

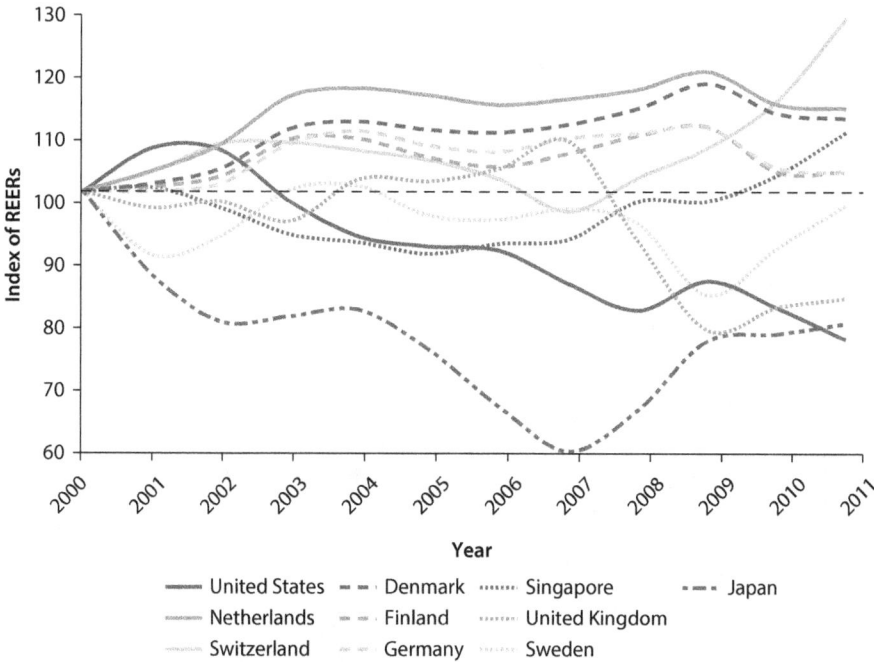

Source: Calculations based on International Monetary Fund, "International Financial Statistics," http://elibrary-data.imf.org/FindDataReports.aspx?d=33061&e=169393.
Note: REERs = real effective exchange rates.

Competitiveness Rankings

A country's competitiveness may be viewed as its competitive position relative to other countries. It has become important for a nation to assess its competitiveness in the increasingly globalized world. A favorable macroeconomic environment is a necessary but insufficient condition for competitiveness; it also matters how productive the nation's enterprises are. Thus, microeconomic factors are critical. Each year, the IMD and the WEF publish rankings of national competitiveness based on macroeconomic and microeconomic factors and subjective assessments by business owners. In addition, the World Bank also publishes the *Doing Business* report. The report ranks countries according to the ease of doing business in their economies. The most recent report (World Bank 2013) covers 11 indicator sets and 183 economies. The following sections examine the competitiveness rankings of countries for 2012 from the reports published by the IMD, WEF, and the World Bank.

World Competitiveness—IMD Rankings
Fifty-nine economies were assessed by the IMD in 2011. Figure 3.2 presents the rankings for the top 20 countries, with the previous year's ranking in parenthesis.

Figure 3.2 World Competitiveness Scoreboard 2011: Top 20 Economies

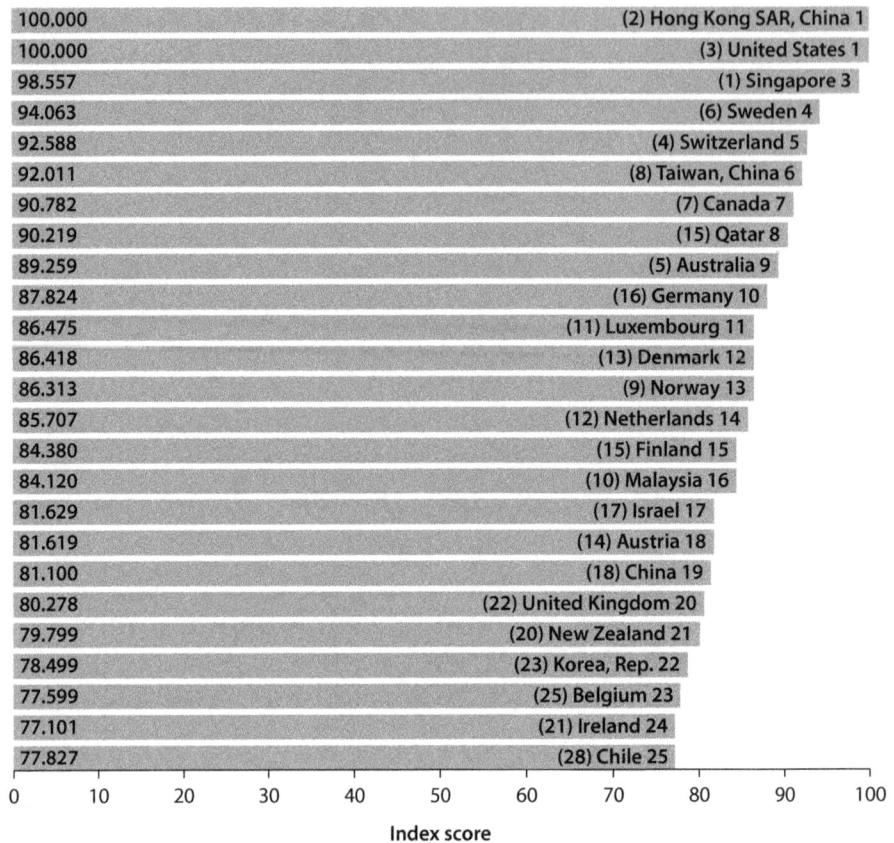

Index score	Economy
100.000	(2) Hong Kong SAR, China 1
100.000	(3) United States 1
98.557	(1) Singapore 3
94.063	(6) Sweden 4
92.588	(4) Switzerland 5
92.011	(8) Taiwan, China 6
90.782	(7) Canada 7
90.219	(15) Qatar 8
89.259	(5) Australia 9
87.824	(16) Germany 10
86.475	(11) Luxembourg 11
86.418	(13) Denmark 12
86.313	(9) Norway 13
85.707	(12) Netherlands 14
84.380	(15) Finland 15
84.120	(10) Malaysia 16
81.629	(17) Israel 17
81.619	(14) Austria 18
81.100	(18) China 19
80.278	(22) United Kingdom 20
79.799	(20) New Zealand 21
78.499	(23) Korea, Rep. 22
77.599	(25) Belgium 23
77.101	(21) Ireland 24
77.827	(28) Chile 25

Index score: 0 10 20 30 40 50 60 70 80 90 100

Source: IMD, http://www.vi.is/files/IMD%202011%20-%20listar_831280280.pdf.
Note: The top 20 of 59 economies ranked by the IMD are shown here, from most to least competitive. The scores shown on the y-axis are indexes (0 to 100) generated for the purpose of constructing charts and graphics.

For the first time since the rankings began, the top position was held jointly by Hong Kong SAR, China, and the United States, which both ranked slightly ahead of Singapore, the top ranked country in 2010. Sweden gained ground and now occupies the 4th position, while Germany gained six places to occupy the 10th position overall. Emerging market countries—for example, Qatar, the Republic of Korea, and Turkey—continue to gain in competitiveness, while the aftereffects of the 2008 global recession leave just four big economies in the top 20. The story behind the ranking suggests a "greater self-reliance of countries. [World competitiveness] increasingly emphasizes re-industrialization, exports, and a more critical look at delocalization."[4]

Competitiveness Trends—The GCI

The GCI has ranked countries since 2005. Figure 3.3 presents an overview of competitiveness trends from 2005 to 2011 for the United States, China, advanced economies, and emerging and developing economies.

Figure 3.3 Competitiveness Trends, 2005–11

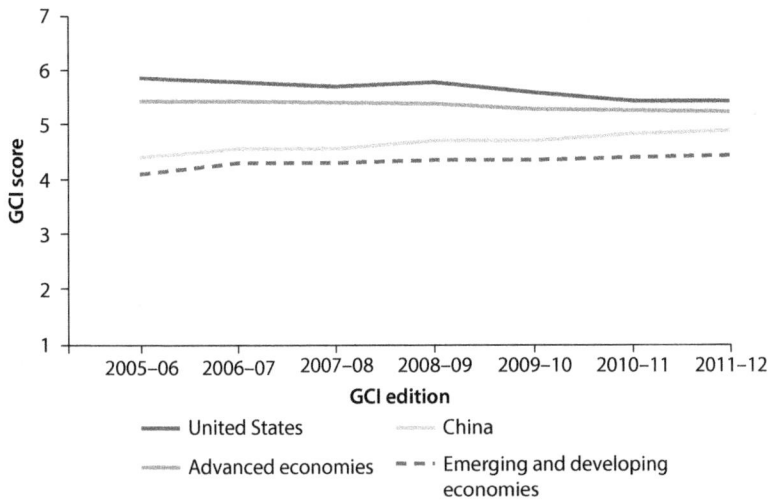

Source: WEF 2012.
Note: GCI = Global Competitiveness Index. The analysis is based on a constant sample composed of the 113 economies already covered in 2005. Country classification is derived from the International Monetary Fund (IMF) and reflects the situation as of April 2011. Weights for the computation of group-weighted averages are based on each economy's share of gross domestic product in its group. Data are taken from IMF, World Economic Outlook, April 2011, http://www.imf.org/external/pubs/ft/weo/2011/01/pdf/text.pdf.

The weighted average overall GCI score is computed for 80 emerging market and developing economies and for 33 advanced economies. There is some convergence of the two groups, but it is gradual. The GCI score for the emerging market and developing economies was 4.1 in 2005, increasing to 4.4 in 2011, while the respective scores for the advanced market economies was 5.4, declining to 5.2. Thus, the spread between the two groups has narrowed from 1.3 to 0.8. The reduction in spread is primarily due to the contrasting experience in China and the United States, the two largest economies. The United States was ranked first overall in 2005, falling to fifth place in 2011. China on the other hand improved its ranking, experiencing a 0.5 increase in its GCI over the study period.

Figure 3.3 suggests a gradual catching up of the emerging and developing economies, with some stagnation among the advanced economies. WEF (2012) notes that four advanced economies suffered a large loss in their GCI score over the study period: the United States (–0.4), Greece (–0.3), and Ireland and Iceland (–0.2 each). However, score loss is not characteristic of all advanced economies—both Switzerland and Sweden have gained 0.3 points since 2005 (WEF 2012).

Table 3.1 examines the ranking for the top 10 countries in 2011–12 and compares this with their ranking between 2005–06 and 2008–09. Switzerland ranked first in 2011–12, followed by Singapore, Sweden, and Finland, with the United States in the fifth position as noted above. Three of these countries

Table 3.1 Global Competitive Index for Top 10 Countries for 2011–12 versus 2005–06 and 2008–09 Rankings

Country/economy	GCI 2011–12		GCI 2005–06	GCI 2008–09
	Rank 1/142	Score	Rank 1/117	Rank 1/134
Switzerland	1	5.74	4	2
Singapore	2	5.63	5	5
Sweden	3	5.61	7	4
Finland	4	5.47	2	6
United States	5	5.43	1	1
Germany	6	5.41	6	7
Netherlands	7	5.41	11	8
Denmark	8	5.40	3	3
Japan	9	5.40	10	9
United Kingdom	10	5.39	9	12

Source: WEF 2006, 2009, 2012.
Note: GCI = Global Competitiveness Index.

(the United States, Switzerland, and Singapore) were in the top five slots in 2005–06 and 2008–09, with Denmark replacing Sweden in 2005–06 and Finland in 2008–09. The ranking has changed over time, with Singapore moving to second place in 2011–12 from fifth place in 2005–06 and 2008–09. Germany and Japan have been consistently ranked in the top 10 for the years chosen, while the Netherlands and the United Kingdom are usually there also.

Examining the country rankings across the 12 pillars of competitiveness outlined in chapter 2 clarifies the GCI score and rankings. As would be expected, all countries score highly on these pillars with some exceptions. Poor macroeconomic stability is an area of weakness for several countries: the United States, which has had repeated fiscal deficits leading to large levels of public indebtedness; the United Kingdom, which had double-digit fiscal deficits in 2010 and a large public debt (77 percent of gross domestic product [GDP] in 2010) coupled with a comparatively low national savings rate (12.3 percent of GDP in 2010); and Japan, which had high budget deficits and the highest public debt of the sample (220 percent of GDP in 2010). Table 3.2 shows the country rankings across the 12 pillars for the top 10 economies.

The *Global Competitiveness Report* identifies five regions—Europe and North America, Asia and the Pacific, Latin America and the Caribbean, the Middle East and North Africa, and Sub-Saharan Africa. There are no regional rankings, but it is possible to identify both top performers and those that have not fared so well among the regional country groupings. The *Global Competitiveness Report* highlights those areas in which there is room for improvement, that is, where a country is underperforming and requires further efforts in order to attain greater competitiveness. As one would expect, the areas for improvement increase as the country rankings decrease. Thus, the economies ranked in the top 40 have few areas for improvement, but once we cross that threshold, the areas for improvement increase. One further point is that not all pillars are relevant, depending on an economy's level of growth and development as captured in the three

Table 3.2 Twelve Pillar Rankings for GCI Top 10 Countries, 2011–12

	Institutions	Infrastructure	Macroeconomic environment	Health and primary education	Higher education and training	Goods market efficiency	Labor market efficiency	Financial market development	Technological readiness	Market size	Business sophistication	Innovation
Switzerland	6	5	7	8	3	5	1	7	1	39	3	1
Singapore	1	3	9	3	4	1	2	1	10	37	15	8
Sweden	2	13	13	18	2	7	25	11	2	31	2	2
Finland	4	19	20	1	1	21	15	9	12	54	9	3
United States	39	16	90	42	13	24	4	22	20	1	10	5
Germany	19	2	30	23	7	26	64	39	14	5	4	7
Netherlands	10	7	36	7	8	9	23	23	5	18	5	12
Denmark	5	10	31	28	6	16	6	17	4	53	6	10
Japan	24	15	113	9	19	18	12	32	25	4	1	4
United Kingdom	15	6	85	14	16	19	7	20	8	6	8	13

Source: WEF 2012.

Note: GCI = Global Competitiveness Index.

categories of basic requirements, efficiency enhancers, and innovation and sophistication factors.

Insufficient or lagging development in institutions is of concern in Italy, Turkey, the Russian Federation, Ukraine, and Greece (table 3.3). Public institutions (government inefficiency, corruption, undue influence) hamper competitiveness in Greece, Turkey, and Italy. Little improvement has occurred in the weak institutional framework in Ukraine and Russia. Rigidities in labor markets and weak financial markets also hamper competitiveness in many of the countries in the Europe and North America region. Labor market concerns include strict hiring and firing rules in France and Spain, rigid labor markets in Italy and Portugal hindering employment creation, a disconnect between salaries and productivity in Portugal and Spain, and inefficient labor markets in Turkey and Greece (table 3.3). Insufficiently developed financial markets in Italy, a low national savings rate in Spain, and a high level of debt in Portugal hinder finance for business development in these countries. Financial markets in Iceland, Greece, and Ireland have been weakened, while Russian markets remain unstable, with poor assessments of the banks. Macroeconomic instability is a threat to competitiveness and a factor adversely affecting the competitiveness rankings in a number of European countries: persistent deficits and high levels of public debt characterize the macroeconomies in Belgium, Ireland, and Spain, and the ongoing sovereign debt crisis in Greece hampers competitiveness on many levels.

Table 3.4 and WEF 2012 examine the competitiveness rankings and underlying pillars in selected economies in Asia and the Pacific region. The disparity in competitiveness rankings is highest in Asia and the Pacific. This region is home to

Table 3.3 GCI and Pillar Rankings for North America and Europe Region, Selected Countries, 2011–12

Country	GCI rank	Pillar											
		1	2	3	4	5	6	7	8	9	10	11	12
Belgium	15	27	17	**60**	2	5	14	44	28	11	26	11	15
France	18	28	4	**83**	16	20	38	**68**	18	13	7	14	17
Ireland	29	23	29	**118**	12	22	13	17	**115**	17	56	22	23
Iceland	30	25	14	**131**	5	9	40	10	**108**	3	**128**	28	19
Spain	36	49	12	**84**	44	32	66	**119**	64	28	13	34	39
Poland	41	52	**74**	74	40	31	52	58	34	48	20	**60**	**58**
Italy	43	88	32	92	20	41	59	**123**	**97**	42	9	26	43
Portugal	45	51	23	**111**	34	35	62	**122**	78	19	45	50	32
Turkey	59	**80**	51	69	**75**	**74**	47	**133**	55	55	17	58	69
Russian Federation	66	**128**	48	44	68	52	**128**	65	**127**	68	8	**114**	**71**
Ukraine	82	**131**	71	**112**	74	51	**129**	61	**116**	82	38	**103**	**74**
Greece	90	**96**	45	**140**	37	46	**107**	**126**	**110**	47	42	77	88

Source: WEF 2012.
Note: Numbers in **bold** type denote areas for improvement. Pillars are as follows: 1= institutions; 2 = infrastructure; 3 = macroeconomic environment; 4 = health and primary education; 5 = higher education and training; 6 = goods market efficiency; 7 = labor market efficiency; 8 = financial market development; 9 = technological readiness; 10 = market size; 11 = business sophistication; 12 = innovation.

Table 3.4 GCI and Pillar Rankings for Asia and the Pacific Region, Selected Economies, 2011–12

Country	GCI rank	Pillar											
		1	2	3	4	5	6	7	8	9	10	11	12
Hong Kong SAR, China	11	9	1	8	**27**	24	3	3	2	6	28	19	**25**
Taiwan, China	13	**31**	20	22	11	10	11	**33**	24	24	16	13	9
Australia	20	13	**24**	26	10	11	22	13	6	22	19	**29**	**22**
Malaysia	21	30	26	29	33	**38**	15	20	3	**44**	29	20	24
Korea, Rep.	24	**65**	9	6	15	17	37	**76**	80	18	11	25	14
China	26	**48**	44	10	32	58	45	36	48	77	2	37	29
Thailand	39	**67**	42	28	83	62	42	30	50	84	22	47	54
India	56	**69**	**89**	105	101	87	70	81	21	93	3	43	38
Indonesia	46	**71**	**76**	23	64	69	67	**94**	69	**94**	15	45	36
Vietnam	65	**87**	**90**	65	73	**103**	75	46	73	79	33	87	66
Philippines	75	**117**	**105**	54	92	71	88	**113**	71	83	36	57	**108**
Pakistan	118	**107**	**115**	**138**	**121**	**122**	**93**	**136**	70	**115**	30	76	75

Source: WEF 2012.

Note: Numbers in **bold** type denote areas for improvement. For pillars, see note to table 3.3. GCI = Global Competitiveness Index.

Singapore, which is ranked 2nd globally, and to Japan, which is ranked 9th, but also to Timor-Leste at 131st. Hong Kong SAR, China, is an anomaly, ranking 11th globally (and third in the region) but featured among the top three in infrastructure (first), goods market (third), labor market (third), and financial market (second). Improving its competitiveness will require a higher participation rate in education and improvements to its innovative capacity. Taiwan, China, is ranked 13th in 2011, a ranking consistent with earlier years. The economy ranks in the top 10 positions in just two of the pillars—education (10th) and innovation (9th). The economy has the largest number of granted patents worldwide (from the United States Patent and Trademark Office) on a per capita basis. It features an excellent education system and a high-end manufacturing sector characterized by high-quality business clusters and research and development (R&D). Two sources of weakness are rigidity in its labor markets and insufficiently developed public and private institutions. Rigidities and labor market inefficiency in Indonesia hamper competitiveness there, with a similar story in the Philippines and Pakistan.

Three areas of concern in Australia are innovation, business sophistication, and infrastructure. The increase in commodity trade in recent years has placed significant demands on its transport infrastructure, and some areas, in particular the seaports, are feeling the strain. The success of the innovation path being pursued by the Malaysian economy depends upon the quality of the education and technological adoption by business and the population in general—two areas of concern.

Concerns about institutions hamper the competitiveness profile of the remaining countries in the sample. The overall quality of institutions was assessed unfavorably in Korea, the Philippines, and Pakistan. Many of the institutional aspects related to business were assessed poorly in the case of China (business ethics, corporate accountability), India and Vietnam (corruption and onerous regulation), and Indonesia (corruption and bribery), while poor public institutions were noted in Thailand. Concerns about infrastructure were also dominant among the sample of countries in this region. In particular, the infrastructure in India is considered grossly inadequate for the country's developmental and growth needs, and the improvements adopted since 2006 have been insufficient. Road transport in Vietnam, port facilities and electricity supply in Indonesia, and air and sea transport in the Philippines are considered lacking, despite improvements, while there has been no sign of improvement in the infrastructure in Pakistan.

The Philippines showed one of the largest improvements in competitiveness in 2012, moving 10 places to a GCI of 75; this gain was achieved by significant improvements in many of the pillars, although as we have noted, many challenges remain.

The Latin America region has rebounded quickly from the 2008 global financial crisis, aided by continuing efforts to maintain macroeconomic stability, high international demand for the region's commodities, and the large internal market (WEF 2012). However, the long-term viability of the recovery is of concern, particularly in light of the region's poor institutional record. Poor institutional quality is identified as a factor hampering competitiveness in 7 of the 12 countries in the regional sample (table 3.5), with República Bolivariana de Venezuela having the worst record in the global sample. Poor quality of public institutions was also identified in Panama and Belize, the first time that Belize has been included in the global sample. The quality of public and private institutions is a cause for concern in Colombia and Argentina, while the improvements made in the private institutions in Mexico and Peru are not matched by similar improvements in public institutions. The second regional cause for concern is the weak record of innovation. Greater achievement in innovation is a necessary factor for economies to move toward higher stages of development. Poor

Table 3.5 GCI and Pillar Rankings for Latin America and the Caribbean Region, Selected Countries, 2011–12

Country	GCI rank	Pillar											
		1	2	3	4	5	6	7	8	9	10	11	12
Chile	31	26	41	14	**71**	43	25	39	37	45	46	39	**46**
Barbados	42	18	22	**126**	17	25	56	35	29	29	**134**	41	49
Panama	49	**75**	38	41	**79**	**78**	46	**115**	27	40	85	46	72
Brazil	53	77	**64**	**115**	87	57	113	**83**	43	54	10	31	44
Mexico	58	**103**	66	39	69	**72**	84	**114**	83	63	12	56	**63**
Costa Rica	61	53	83	**109**	39	47	57	55	**91**	56	83	35	35
Uruguay	63	35	49	**59**	47	42	77	118	79	49	87	83	55
Peru	67	**95**	88	52	**97**	77	50	43	38	69	48	65	**113**
Colombia	68	**100**	**85**	42	78	60	99	88	68	75	32	61	57
Argentina	85	**134**	81	62	56	54	**137**	131	126	64	24	79	78
Belize	123	**120**	**100**	88	53	**112**	**121**	82	**111**	**118**	**140**	116	135
Venezuela, RB	124	**142**	117	128	84	**67**	**142**	**142**	**132**	92	41	**124**	**126**

Source: WEF 2012.
Note: Numbers in **bold** type denote areas for improvement. For pillars, see note to table 3.3. GCI = Global Competitiveness Index.

performance on the innovation pillar was noted as a cause for concern in Chile, Peru, Mexico, and República Bolivariana de Venezuela. The potential for progress on the innovation pillar is stymied by poor rankings on the education pillar in Chile, Mexico, and Peru. Although República Bolivariana de Venezuela boasts an impressive tertiary education enrollment rate, the overall quality of education is weak and hinders the innovation potential of the country.

Figure 3.4 examines the trends in the innovation pillar score and compares the Latin America region with the Organisation for Economic Co-operation and Development (OECD) average and China. The stable performance of Latin America has remained below the OECD average and has failed to converge on the more developed economies, in contrast to China. The *Global Competitiveness Report* calls for "a higher allocation of public and private resources toward education and training activities and R&D" (WEF 2012, 35).

The competitiveness rankings in the Middle East and North Africa region suggest a divide between the Gulf economies and the others. The competitiveness gap may be further exacerbated by the political and social turbulence from early 2011 (WEF 2012). The rankings depicted in table 3.6 were assembled before the period termed the Arab Spring occurred, except in the case of the Arab Republic of Egypt and Tunisia. Both economies suffered in their rankings, with Egypt dropping 13 places and Tunisia 8 places. The Republic of Yemen was added to the global sample in 2011 and was ranked 138th.

Qatar was ranked the most competitive in the region, on the back of strong macroeconomic performance, business sophistication, and innovation. The financial sector is an area of concern noted by the business community, which is apprehensive about the soundness of the banking system and the unprotected

Figure 3.4 Trends in the GCI Innovation Pillar Score, 2005–11

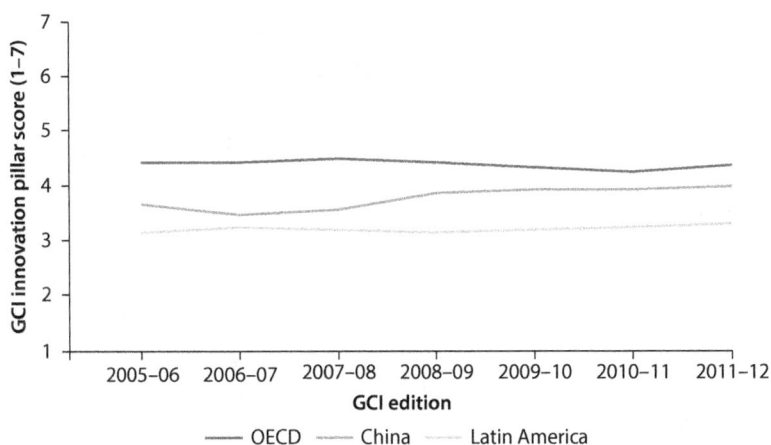

Source: WEF 2012.
Note: The Latin American average includes Argentina, Barbados, Chile, Colombia, Costa Rica, Mexico, Panama, Peru, Puerto Rico, and Uruguay. Together these countries represent more than 90 percent of the regional gross domestic product. GCI = Global Competitiveness Index; OECD = Organisation for Economic Co-operation and Development.

Table 3.6 GCI and Pillar Rankings for Middle East and North Africa Region, Selected Countries, 2011–12

Country	GCI rank	Pillar											
		1	2	3	4	5	6	7	8	9	10	11	12
Qatar	14	14	27	5	22	50	17	22	19	33	59	12	18
Saudi Arabia	17	12	25	12	**61**	**36**	4	**50**	16	**43**	23	17	26
Israel	22	**33**	53	**53**	**36**	27	33	24	10	21	51	16	6
United Arab Emirates	27	**22**	8	11	41	33	10	28	33	30	43	23	28
Tunisia	40	**41**	52	38	38	44	44	**106**	76	58	63	52	37
Egypt, Arab Rep.	94	74	75	**132**	96	**107**	118	**141**	92	95	27	72	103
Yemen, Rep.	138	**140**	**132**	**130**	**127**	**138**	**133**	**129**	**142**	**139**	78	**134**	**142**

Source: WEF 2012.
Note: Numbers in **bold** type denote areas for improvement. For pillars, see note to table 3.3. GCI = Global Competitiveness Index.

Table 3.7 GCI and Pillar Scores—Sub-Saharan Africa, Selected Countries, 2011

Country	GCI rank	Pillar											
		1	2	3	4	5	6	7	8	9	10	11	12
South Africa	50	**46**	**62**	55	**131**	**73**	32	**95**	4	76	25	38	**41**
Mauritius	54	40	54	79	55	**68**	28	**67**	42	61	110	44	89
Rwanda	70	21	**101**	61	**112**	**119**	49	8	54	109	129	84	56
Botswana	80	32	92	**82**	**120**	**93**	68	52	44	101	99	101	79
Namibia	83	43	58	63	**114**	113	71	57	36	**99**	120	95	92
Kenya	102	**114**	103	117	**118**	94	80	37	26	98	77	59	52
Ghana	114	61	110	**139**	**124**	109	72	**79**	61	**113**	81	99	98
Tanzania	120	85	**130**	129	**113**	**131**	112	73	85	**126**	82	104	73
Nigeria	127	**111**	**135**	121	**140**	114	73	70	86	**106**	34	64	62
Zimbabwe	132	**97**	127	**136**	**123**	118	**124**	**130**	104	128	133	120	117

Source: WEF 2012.
Note: Numbers in **bold** type denote areas for improvement. GCI = Global Competitiveness Index.

rights of lenders and borrowers. The institutions pillar is a cause of concern in the majority of the countries surveyed, from security concerns in Israel, to corruption, government favoritism, and a judiciary that is less independent than in the past in Tunisia. Institutional rankings have also fallen in the United Arab Emirates perhaps due to the severity of the economic crisis there (WEF 2012), and the Republic of Yemen has a very weak institutional framework—public and private. Poor outcomes for health and education, pillar 4, hamper competitiveness in the Republic of Yemen and Saudi Arabia, while the quality of education and the poor representation in the math and science areas are cause for concern in Israel. Labor market rigidities and inefficiencies adversely affect competitiveness in Egypt and Saudi Arabia.

Countries in Sub-Saharan Africa lag behind the rest of the world in competitiveness, and many areas of concern are noted in table 3.7. South Africa and Mauritius are top ranked in the region, but even here a number of pillars require further effort, especially in South Africa. Pillar 4, health and primary education, is a main area of concern for almost all of the countries; in particular, poor health and the high rate of communicable diseases are issues in this region. The higher education pillar is also difficult for a number of countries. South Africa, for example, has a university enrollment rate of just 15 percent, and enrollment rates and overall quality are judged as insufficient in Mauritius, Rwanda, and Botswana. Tanzania, with commendable primary enrollment rates, has the lowest rates of secondary and tertiary enrollment in the world (WEF 2012). Rigidities and inefficiencies in the labor market constrain competitiveness in South Africa, Mauritius, Ghana, and Zimbabwe. Despite improvements in the institutions pillar in South Africa, Kenya, and Nigeria, security concerns remain a factor and present an obstacle to doing business in these countries. In addition, insufficient protection of property rights is an issue in Zimbabwe and Nigeria. A number of countries are not making sufficient use of technologies to improve productivity; for example, adoption rates for information and communication technology are very low in Ghana, Nigeria, and Tanzania, with low rates of mobile phone penetration in Namibia and Tanzania.

The *Global Competitiveness Report* summarizes the 2011 country rankings by noting the complexity that characterizes national competitiveness, dependent as it is upon an "an array of reforms in different areas that affect the longer-term productivity of a country" (WEF 2012, 44). The rankings facilitate the prioritizing of policy reforms as each country can identify its own strengths and weaknesses in achieving economic growth, development, and competitiveness.

In the past, both the IMD's *World Competitiveness Yearbook* and the WEF's *Global Competitiveness Report* have been criticized for their methodology and the subjectivity of their findings (Lall 2001). Arguably the changes in methodology that these two publications have imposed throughout their life span have addressed the criticisms.

Doing Business *Report*

The World Bank/International Finance Corporation publication *Doing Business* also ranks countries according to the regulatory practices pertaining to small- and medium-size companies. Now in its 10th year, the *Doing Business* report provides an important insight to trends in regulatory reform. The main findings from the 2013 report indicate the following:

- Smarter business regulation supports economic growth.
- Simpler business registration promotes greater entrepreneurship and firm productivity.
- Lower-cost registration improves formal employment opportunities.
- An effective regulatory environment boosts trade performance.
- Sound financial market infrastructure—courts, creditor and insolvency laws, and credit and collateral registries—improves access to credit (World Bank 2013).

Clusters of Competitiveness • http://dx.doi.org/10.1596/978-1-4648-0049-8

Table 3.8 Top 10 Economies for Ease of Doing Business in 2013, versus 2012 and 2011 Rankings

Economy	Rank 2013	Rank 2012	Rank 2011
Singapore	1	1	1
Hong Kong SAR, China	2	2	2
New Zealand	3	3	3
United States	4	4	4
Denmark	5	5	5
Norway	6	6	7
United Kingdom	7	7	6
Korea, Rep.	8	8	15
Georgia	9	16	17
Australia	10	15	11

Source: World Bank 2012, 2013.

The aggregate ranking on the ease of doing business for small- and medium-size companies in 185 countries is based on indicator sets for 10 areas of the firms' life cycles.[5] The indicator sets measure and benchmark regulations in these areas: starting a business, dealing with construction permits, getting electricity, registering property, getting credit, protecting investors, paying taxes, trading across borders, enforcing contracts, and resolving insolvency (World Bank 2013).

Table 3.8 presents the top 10 countries ranked by ease of doing business for 2013 and compares their ranks in the previous 2 years. There has been no change in the top five economies over the period, with Singapore in the number 1 position, followed by Hong Kong SAR, China; New Zealand; the United States; and Denmark. Georgia moved from a rank of 17th in 2011 to 16th in 2012 and to 9th in 2013. Australia also made similar strides upward between 2012 and 2013, and Korea also progressed through the rankings. A number 1 ranking does not imply that the country ranked first in all of the 10 indicators. The ease of doing business is an aggregate measure, an average of the 10 indicators identified above. Figure 3.5 illustrates the dispersion around the average. Thus, any conclusions from table 3.8 should also take into account the dispersion across the measures. For example, Singapore's rankings range from 1 in trading across borders to 36 in registering property.

The *Doing Business* report notes that 58 percent of the surveyed countries implemented at least one institutional or regulatory reform, making it easier to do business; 23 countries implemented reforms in three or more areas. Of these 23 countries, 10 moved ahead quite significantly through the rankings (table 3.9).

The 10 indicators underlying the aggregate "ease of doing business" can be classified into two groups—a group that summarizes the strength of legal institutions relevant to business regulation and a group that illustrates the complexity and costs of regulatory processes. The two sets of indicators form the axes in figure 3.6. Regions in the figure's northeast quadrant combine strong legal institutions and business-friendly regulation, whereas regions in the southwest quadrant have weak legal institutions and the least business-friendly regulation.

Figure 3.5 Variation in Individual Economies' Regulatory Environment (dispersion around average)

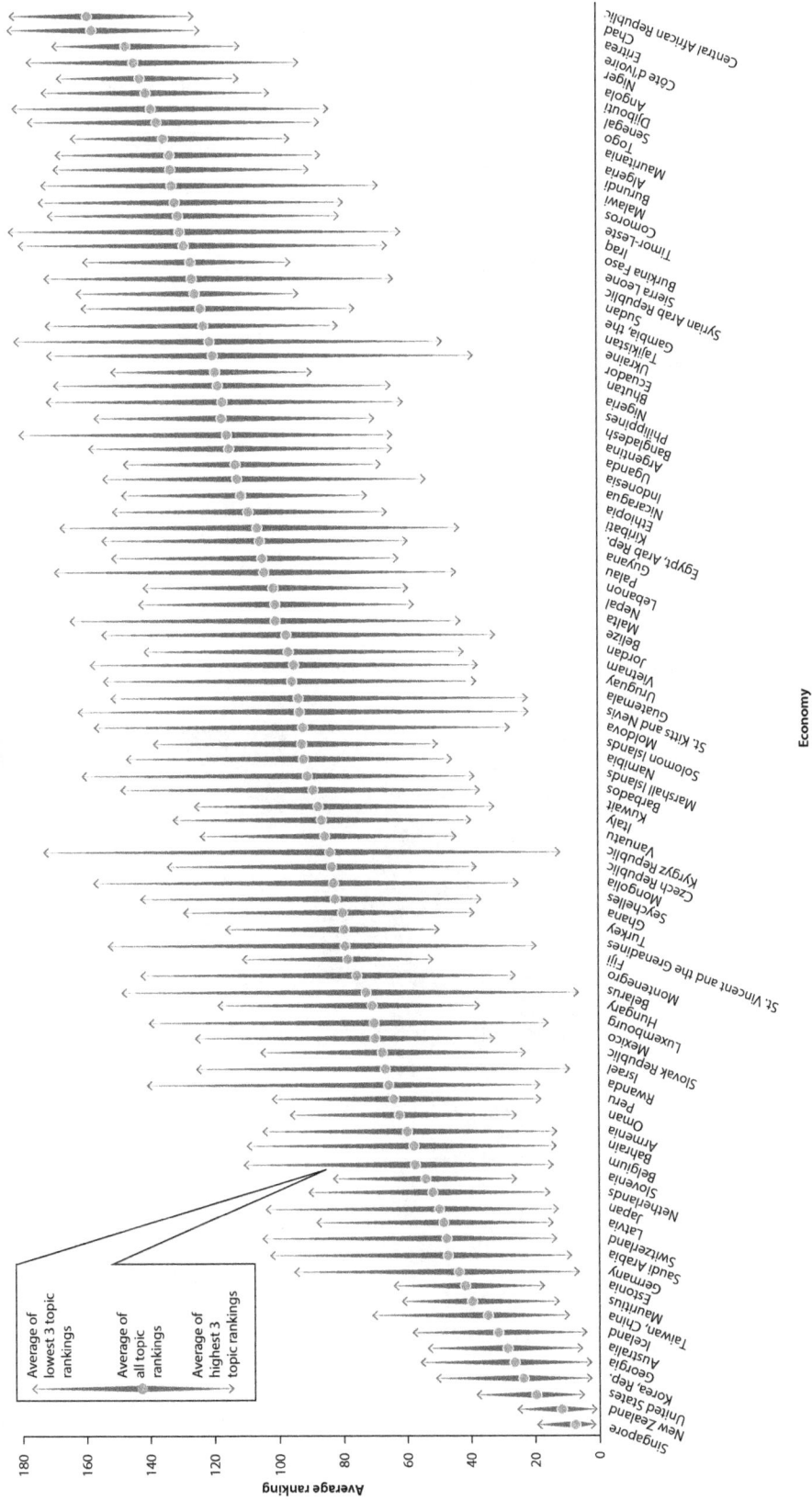

Average ranking (y-axis): 0, 20, 40, 60, 80, 100, 120, 140, 160, 180

Legend:
- Average of lowest 3 topic rankings
- Average of all topic rankings
- Average of highest 3 topic rankings

Economy (x-axis, from left): Singapore, New Zealand, United States, Korea, Rep., Georgia, Australia, Iceland, Taiwan, China, Mauritius, Estonia, Germany, Saudi Arabia, Switzerland, Latvia, Japan, Netherlands, Slovenia, Belgium, Bahrain, Armenia, Oman, Peru, Rwanda, Israel, Slovak Republic, Mexico, Luxembourg, Hungary, Belarus, Montenegro, Fiji, St. Vincent and the Grenadines, Turkey, Seychelles, Ghana, Mongolia, Czech Republic, Kyrgyz Republic, Vanuatu, Italy, Kuwait, Barbados, Marshall Islands, Namibia, Solomon Islands, Moldova, St. Kitts and Nevis, Guatemala, Uruguay, Vietnam, Jordan, Belize, Malta, Nepal, Lebanon, Palau, Guyana, Egypt, Arab Rep., Kiribati, Ethiopia, Nicaragua, Indonesia, Uganda, Argentina, Bangladesh, Philippines, Nigeria, Bhutan, Ecuador, Ukraine, Tajikistan, Gambia, the, Sudan, Syrian Arab Republic, Sierra Leone, Burkina Faso, Iraq, Timor-Leste, Comoros, Malawi, Burundi, Algeria, Mauritania, Togo, Senegal, Djibouti, Angola, Niger, Côte d'Ivoire, Eritrea, Chad, Central African Republic

Source: World Bank 2013.

71

Table 3.9 Ten Economies Showing Most Improvement in Ease of Doing Business, 2011–13

Economy	2011 Rank	2012 Rank	2013 Rank
Poland	59	62	55
Sri Lanka	98	89	81
Ukraine	149	152	137
Uzbekistan	164	166	154
Burundi	177	169	159
Costa Rica	121	121	110
Mongolia	89	86	76
Greece	101	100	78
Serbia	88	92	86
Kazakhstan	58	47	49

Source: World Bank 2013, 2012.
Note: The economies shown improved in three or more areas as measured by Doing Business.

Figure 3.6 Regions Ranked by Strength of Legal Institutions and Complexity and Cost of Regulatory Processes

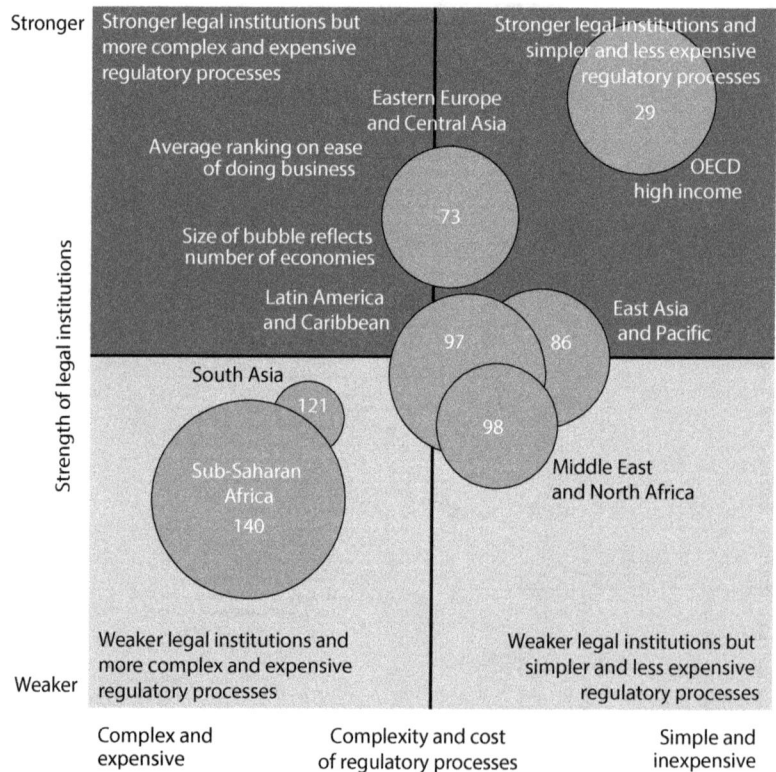

Source: World Bank 2013, 4.
Note: OECD = Organisation for Economic Co-operation and Development.

Figure 3.6 shows the OECD and other high-income economies in the northeast quadrant, with an average rank of doing business of 29. The Middle East and North Africa region and the East Asia and Pacific region have quite efficient regulatory processes but lag behind when it comes to the strength of their legal institutions. The Latin America and the Caribbean region is also part of this group. The Eastern Europe and Central Asia region has fairly strong legal institutions but more complex and expensive regulatory processes. By comparison, Sub-Saharan Africa and South Asia have weaker legal institutions and more complex and expensive regulatory processes.

Business regulation reform has an impact on economic outcomes. With more years of data now available, it is possible to examine the impact of business regulation reform on a number of variables, although "credibly pinning down the magnitude of this effect is more difficult" (World Bank 2013, 11). Low-income countries that implemented reforms over a 5-year period experienced an increase in their growth rate of 0.4 percentage points in the following year (World Bank 2013).

Figure 3.7 shows the effect of business regulatory reform on business start-up. This area of research has increased in recent years and has shown that "simpler entry regulations encourage the creation of more new firms and new jobs in the formal sector" (World Bank 2013, 11). Figure 3.7 shows noticeable increases in business registrations after reforms have taken place.

The *Doing Business* report provides valuable insights for policy makers and planners on the state of business regulation reform across countries. Now in its

Figure 3.7 Impact of Regulatory Reform on Registration of New Firms

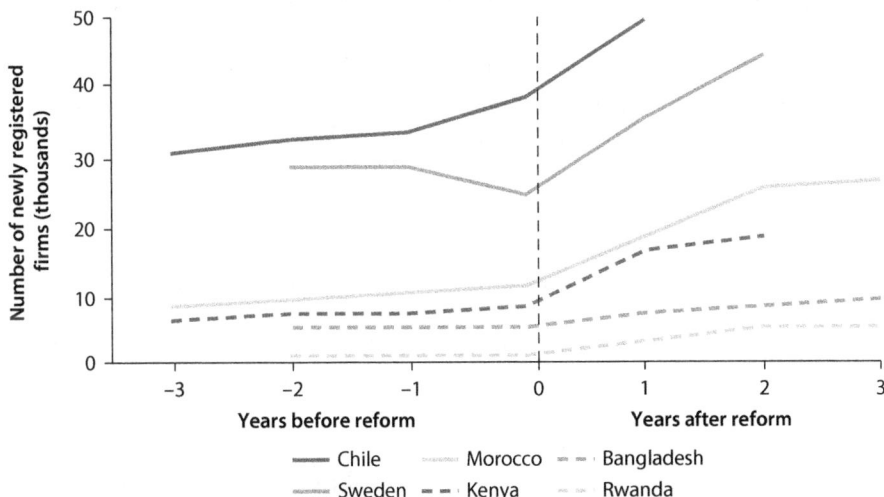

Legend: Chile, Morocco, Bangladesh, Sweden, Kenya, Rwanda

x-axis: Years before reform (−3, −2, −1, 0), Years after reform (0, 1, 2, 3)
y-axis: Number of newly registered firms (thousands) (0, 10, 20, 30, 40, 50)

Source: World Bank 2013.
Note: All 6 economies implemented a reform making it easier to start a business as measured by *Doing Business.* The reform years vary by economy and are represented by the vertical line in the figure. For Bangladesh and Rwanda, it is 2009; for Chile, 2011; for Kenya, 2007; for Morocco, 2006; and for Sweden, 2010.

Clusters of Competitiveness • http://dx.doi.org/10.1596/978-1-4648-0049-8

10th year, it has amassed a wealth of data that can be combined with other variables to show the economic impact of business regulatory reforms.

Conclusion

The chapter looked at competitiveness rankings across countries. The two main sources are the annual publications from the IMD and the WEF. We looked also at the annual *Doing Business* report from the World Bank. The latter provides insight into business regulation and reforms. The GCI from the WEF has the largest coverage in terms of countries and indicators. Data are gathered for 12 pillars that summarize all aspects of the macroeconomy and microeconomy and that result in an overall ranking, the GCI. Switzerland occupied the top position in 2011–2012, while the United States, after 2 years in the number 1 position, moved to number 5.

Notes

1. The other well-known published ranking is the index prepared by the International Institute for Management Development (IMD) discussed below. There are many unpublished reports "prepared by governments, consultants, and research institutions" (Lall 2001, 1501).

2. Bakardzhieva, Ben Naceur, and Kamar (2010) cite Eyraud (2009), Bennett and Zarnic (2008), and Monfort (2008).

3. This explanation is from the Organisation for Economic Co-operation and Development, "Glossary of Statistical Terms," http://stats.oecd.org/glossary/detail. asp?ID=2243.

4. The quotation is from Stéphane Garelli, in IMD, "IMD Announces the 2011 World Competitiveness Rankings and the Results of the 'Government Efficiency Gap.'" Press release, May 17. 2011. http://www.imd.org/news/IMD-announces-the-2011-World-Competitiveness-Rankings-and-the-results-of-the-Government-Efficiency-Gap.cfm.

5. The *Doing Business* report also includes regulations on employing workers, which is not included in the 2013 aggregate ranking (World Bank 2013).

References

Bakardzhieva, D., S. Ben Naceur, and B. Kamar. 2010. "The Impact of Capital and Foreign Exchange Flows on the Competitiveness of Developing Countries." Working Paper WP/10/154, International Monetary Fund, Washington, DC.

Bennett, H., and Z. Zarnic. 2008. "International Competitiveness of the Mediterranean Quarter: A Heterogeneous-Product Approach." Working Paper WP/08/240, International Monetary Fund, Washington, DC.

Eyraud, L. 2009. "Madagascar: A Competitiveness and Exchange Rate Assessment." IMF Working Paper WP/09/107, International Monetary Fund, Washington, DC.

Garelli, S. 2011. "The Fundamentals and History of Competitiveness." In *IMD World Competitiveness Yearbook 2011*, Appendix 3. Lausanne, Switzerland: International Institute for Management Development.

IMD (International Institute for Management Development). 2011. "IMD Announces the 2011 World Competitiveness Rankings and the Results of the 'Government Efficiency Gap.'" Press release, May 17, 2011. http://www.imd.org/news/IMD-announces-the-2011-World-Competitiveness-Rankings-and-the-results-of-the-Government-Efficiency-Gap.cfm.

———. 2012. *IMD World Competitiveness Yearbook 2012*. Lausanne, Switzerland: IMD.

IMF (International Monetary Fund). "International Financial Statistics, IFS—IMF eLibrary Data." http://elibrary-data.imf.org/FindDataReports.aspx?d=33061&e=169393.

Krugman, P. 1994. "Competitiveness—A Dangerous Obsession." *Foreign Affairs* 73 (2): 28–44. http://www.pkarchive.org/global/pop.html.

Lall, S. 2001. "Competitiveness Indices and Developing Countries: An Economic Evaluation of the Global Competitiveness Report." *World Development Report* 29 (9): 1501–25.

Monfort, B. 2008. "Chile: Trade Performance, Trade Liberalization, and Competitiveness." Working Paper WP/08/128, International Monetary Fund, Washington, DC.

WEF (World Economic Forum). 2006. *The Global Competitiveness Report 2005–2006*. Geneva: World Economic Forum.

———. 2009. *The Global Competitiveness Report 2008–2009*. Geneva: World Economic Forum.

———. 2012. *The Global Competitiveness Report 2012–2013*. Geneva: World Economic Forum.

World Bank. 2012. *Doing Business 2012: Doing Business in a More Transparent World*. Washington, DC: World Bank.

———. 2013. *Doing Business 2013: Smarter Regulations for Small and Medium-Size Enterprises*. Washington, DC: World Bank.

CHAPTER 4

Innovation Policy for Competitiveness

The pursuit of competitiveness through innovation is a hallmark of the modern knowledge-driven, globalized economy, primarily in the developed world but also extending to the developing economies wishing to catch up. Innovation is the basis of sustainable economic growth and a key driver of competitiveness. It also plays an important role in promoting economic convergence, increasing welfare, creating new jobs, and destroying old ones. The effects of innovation and competitiveness translate into economic growth at the macroeconomic level. Innovation and competitiveness have thus become major objectives of national policy. An understanding of the factors affecting the innovative efforts of firms and industries and the interactions among these is critical to informing policy for innovation and competitiveness.

Innovation drives competitiveness at many levels—the firm, groups of firms in an industry, the region, and the nation—with substantial scope for interaction across these levels. The increasing interaction among firms—the "death of distance"—arises from interfirm knowledge flows.[1] Knowledge has become easier to share and adopt because of globalization that has been driven by technological change and rapid advances in new technologies such as information and communication technologies (ICTs). Globalization and ICTs have facilitated new forms of competition and opened new markets for innovative products and services. Government, universities, and alliances among companies contribute to the codification of knowledge, that is, available to all, a process that increasingly benefits from ICT.

Following an examination of the definition and measurement of innovation, the chapter highlights some examples of the positive relationship between innovation, economic growth, and competitiveness. Drawing on that discussion, it then examines the elements of an effective innovation policy.

Innovation: Definition and Measurements

The increasing importance ascribed to innovation as a key driver of growth and competitiveness has refocused attention on how this concept is defined and measured. A broader concept of innovation extends to the nature, role, and determinants of innovation and moves beyond the simple definition that focused primarily on the introduction of a new product or a new process, for example. Furthermore, in terms of measuring innovation, efforts have moved beyond a focus on spending for research and development (R&D) to large-scale statistical surveys that measure how firms innovate.[2]

"Innovation is the implementation of a new or significantly improved product (good or service), or process, a new marketing method, or a new organizational method in business practices, workplace organization or external relations" (Organisation for Economic Co-operation and Development [OECD] 2009, 12). This definition arose from innovation surveys that have been carried out by the OECD since 1992. It has been modified twice to reflect the changing nature of innovation. Initially, the innovation surveys were confined to firms in the manufacturing sector and described product and process innovations, but they later evolved to cover service firms and organizational and marketing innovations, resulting in the identification of four types of innovation: product, process, marketing, and organizational. The blueprint for the innovation surveys is the Oslo Manual,[3] which has been adopted in the European Union, Japan, the Republic of Korea, Mexico, New Zealand, Norway, Switzerland, Turkey, the Russian Federation, South Africa, and most of Latin America, though not in the United States (OECD 2009, 12).

The Oslo Manual contends that innovation can be "new to the firm, new to the market or new to the world" (OECD 2010, 1). An innovation new to a firm may already be in place in other firms. New to the market suggests that a new product or process is being introduced to its market for the first time, and new to the world indicates that the innovation is new to all markets and industries. This concept of innovation suggests a much broader notion than that encapsulated by R&D activity (see figure 4.1). Figure 4.1 illustrates that new-to-market product innovators are a feature of innovative firms that have in-house R&D but also firms that do not have in-house R&D. Furthermore, a broader interpretation of innovation suggests greater scope for policy, as innovation is not just about R&D but also extends to "organizational changes, training, testing, marketing and design" (OECD 2010, 1).

The innovation surveys collect information on the firms' inputs and outputs, tangibles and intangibles that relate to their innovative activities. The surveys also capture details about the nature of innovation in each firm, concentrating on R&D, collaboration and links with other firms or public research organizations, the sources of knowledge, the reason for innovating, and the obstacles to innovation. Table 4.1 suggests some simple innovation indicators that may be derived from innovation surveys based on the Oslo Manual.

Figure 4.1 New-to-Market Product Innovators as a Percentage of Innovative Firms by R&D Status, 2004–06

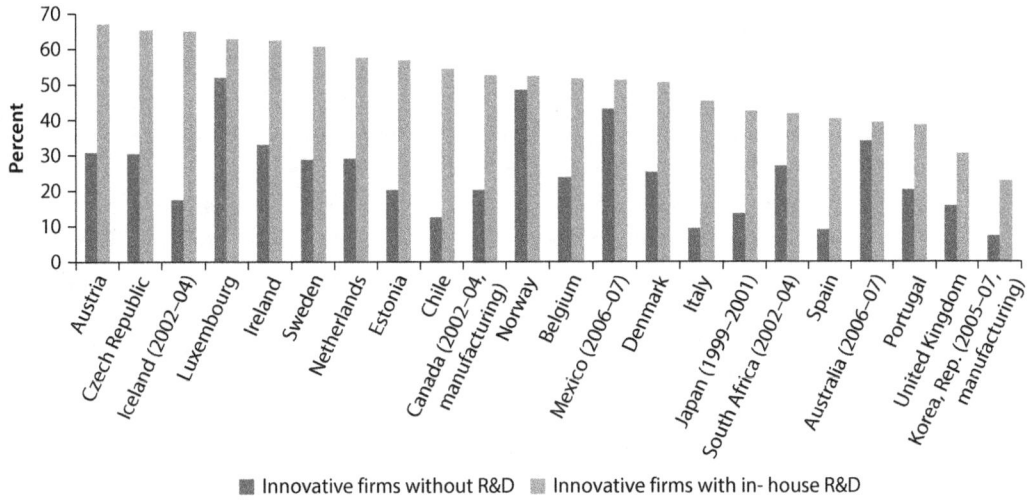

Source: OECD 2010.
Note: R&D = research and development; OECD = Organisation for Economic Co-operation and Development.

Table 4.1 Simple Innovation Indicators

Type of innovation	Indicator(s)
Technological innovation	Share of firms that introduced a product innovation
	Share of firms that introduced a process innovation
	Share of firms that introduced either a product or a process innovation ("innovative firms")
	Share of firms that developed in-house technological innovations (product or process)
	Share of firms that introduced a new-to-market product innovation
Nontechnological innovation	Share of firms that introduced a marketing innovation
	Share of firms that introduced an organizational innovation
	Share of firms that introduced a nontechnological innovation (marketing or organization)
Inputs	Total expenditure on innovation (as percentage of total turnover)
	Expenditure on innovation by type of expenditure (machinery acquisition, external knowledge, R&D, etc.; as percentage of total expenditure on innovation)
	Share of firms that performed R&D
	Share of firms that performed R&D on a continuous basis
Outputs	Share of turnover from product innovation (as percentage of turnover)
	Share of turnover from new-to-market product innovations (as percenatge of turnover)
Key policy-relevant characteristics	Share of firms that were active on international markets (outside the home country)
	Share of firms that cooperated with foreign partners on innovation
	Share of firms that cooperated on innovation activities
	Share of firms that cooperated with universities/higher education or government research institutes
	Share of firms that received public financial support for innovation
	Share of firms that applied for one or more patents (to protect innovations)

Source: OECD 2009.
Note: R&D = research and development; OECD = Organisation for Economic Co-operation and Development.

The first group of indicators in table 4.1 has to do with technological innovation and specifically with product and process innovation. Technology lies behind product and process innovations, whether these have been developed in house or outside the firm. Technological innovation captures both the product and process innovation activities in the firm. Product innovations are the final commercialization of innovation, while process innovations represent improvements in firms' internal processes, as a result of either knowledge acquired through new technology or in-house developments (OECD 2009). The final two indicators in this group differentiate between creative activities and diffusion. The latter derives from in-house technological innovations, while the former captures inventive activity through the introduction of a new product or process.

The second group of indicators, nontechnological innovations, summarizes the marketing and organizational innovations. These areas suggest a much broader concept of innovation and provide scope for policy intervention.

The third group shows measures of innovation inputs, including expenditure on innovation by type of innovation that allows us to differentiate between creative activities, knowledge being developed in house versus knowledge being acquired externally, and R&D expenditures. The input measures differentiate between ongoing expenditures on R&D and expenditures confined to a specific sector for a specific period (intramural).

The fourth group captures output measures of innovation—those that measure the output of any product innovations and those that measure the output of product innovations new to the market.

The final group comprises indicators that focus on internationalization and are directly relevant for policy. Participation in foreign markets and efforts to access international knowledge are both vital for maintaining and increasing competitiveness.

Data from the innovation surveys provide valuable information for the design of innovation policy. The indicators reflect a focus on internationalization that is critical for competitiveness, and also on firms' interaction with other firms, research organizations, government, and universities. Intellectual property rights are a prime focus of policy and are reflected in the patent indicator listed in the last row of table 4.1.

Each indicator by itself conveys information about innovation in each country—that is, one can ascertain the share of firms in each country with a product or process innovation.[4] Of greater interest, particularly to policy makers, are the composite indicators that classify and distinguish different types of innovative firms. Composite indicators combine answers to several questions and provide a better measure of the diversity of innovation taking place within the enterprise. OECD (2009) identifies four composite indicators based on the indicators identified in table 4.1:

- *Output-based innovation modes* classify innovative firms according to the novelty of their innovations and whether innovation was conducted in house or mainly by others.[5]

- *Innovation status* classifies firms according to the inventiveness of their innovation activities and whether they engage in collaboration.[6]
- *Technological and nontechnological innovation* examines the combination of product-process innovation with organizational and marketing innovations.[7]
- *Dual innovators* identify firms that are active in both goods and service innovations.[8]

These composite indicators can be used for benchmarking purposes, although one needs to be aware of the limitations of the data. The surveys are not fully harmonized across the participating countries and the responses may be subject to interpretation differences. Moreover, further work needs to be done to ascertain the statistical significance of the differences in data across countries.

However, indicators derived from innovation surveys have not featured that strongly in policy. R&D indicators are still the most widely used. OECD (2009) cites a number of reasons why this continues to be the case, including the reliability of R&D measures, their role in national science and technology policies, their wide acceptance as an indicator of innovation, and the lack of international comparability across the innovation surveys. That said, the composite indicators derived from the innovation surveys provide a detailed picture of economy-wide innovation activities within the firm and significantly broaden the scope for policy to assist innovative efforts at the level of the firm and the economy.

Innovation, Growth, and Competitiveness

World Bank (2010) states that innovation has always been a key part of economic and social development, and it refers to four key effects of innovation: "It is the main source of economic growth, it helps improve productivity, it is the foundation of competitiveness, and it improves welfare" (World Bank 2010, 6).

Petrakos, Arvanitidis, and Pavleas (2007) refer to the strong association between innovation and economic growth, citing the work of Fagerberg (1987), Lichtenberg (1992), and Ulku (2004) in this regard. Including innovation as a regressor in the empirical models of growth improves the explanatory power of these models. Innovation increases productivity and growth through improved technology arising from new products and processes. Moreover, endogenous growth theory maintains that investment in innovation, human capital, and knowledge results in economic growth, as expressed by

$$Q = f(K, L, \text{R\&D}, \text{HC}),$$

where Q = output, K = capital, L = labor, R&D proxies for innovation, and HC proxies for human capital.

The endogenous growth equation proves a better approximation for growth in developed economies. Developing economies "do not do much R&D" and produce new products and processes by importing the knowledge from developed economies (World Bank 2010, 41). Growth equations in developing

Table 4.2 Extent of Economic Growth beyond Growth Predicted by Rates of Capital Accumulation, Selected Economies, 1960–89

Economy	Investment/GDP (%)	Actual minus predicated growth rate of GDP per capita
Algeria	35.0	−0.026
Gabon	40.0	−0.030
Greece	24.2	0.008
Hong Kong SAR, China	27.3	0.031
Ireland	22.2	0.011
Jamaica	25.0	−0.037
Korea, Rep.	24.9	0.032
Panama	24.0	0.002
Portugal	23.7	−0.002
Singapore	34.3	0.017
Taiwan, China	25.0	0.047

Source: Nelson and Pack 1999; cited in Cantwell 2005.
Note: GDP = gross domestic product.

economies should therefore include imports of capital goods and components as well as foreign direct investment (FDI). Knowledge affects total factor productivity (TFP), that is, the residual for the growth in output not explained by the growth in factor inputs.

Part of capital accumulation derives from the innovative efforts of the firm. Nelson and Pack (1999)[9] show that countries that sustained high rates of capital accumulation, that is, investment in gross domestic product (GDP) of 20 percent or more, achieved growth rates of GDP in excess of what might have been expected from the rates of capital accumulation alone. Table 4.2 shows 11 countries that had high rates of investment to GDP over the 1960 to 1989 period. The right-hand column shows the residuals from a regression of 101 countries of GDP per capita on investment share, the initial level of GDP per capita in 1960 (a proxy for a catching-up effect), the growth of population (to capture the availability of labor supplies), and the relevant cohort of population educated to at least secondary school standards.

The results show that the East Asian countries and economies—Hong Kong SAR, China; Korea; Singapore; and Taiwan, China—achieved growth rates in excess of what might have been expected, given their favorable rates of capital accumulation. Cantwell (2005, 7) suggests that what was different in these economies "was their greater ability to innovate, to upgrade and restructure their indigenous industries, and to learn and absorb more effectively from foreign technologies."

In addition to these studies, the growth literature that focuses on cross-country convergence, or catching up, identifies innovation as a key factor in explaining differences across countries. Figure 4.2 shows how innovation contributed to growth in two countries—Ghana and Korea—from 1960 to 2005. The disparity in growth performance was primarily due to TFP or knowledge accumulation (figure 4.2).[10] Roughly two-thirds of the difference in output between the two countries was

Figure 4.2 Contribution of Innovation to Growth in Ghana and the Republic of Korea, 1960–2005

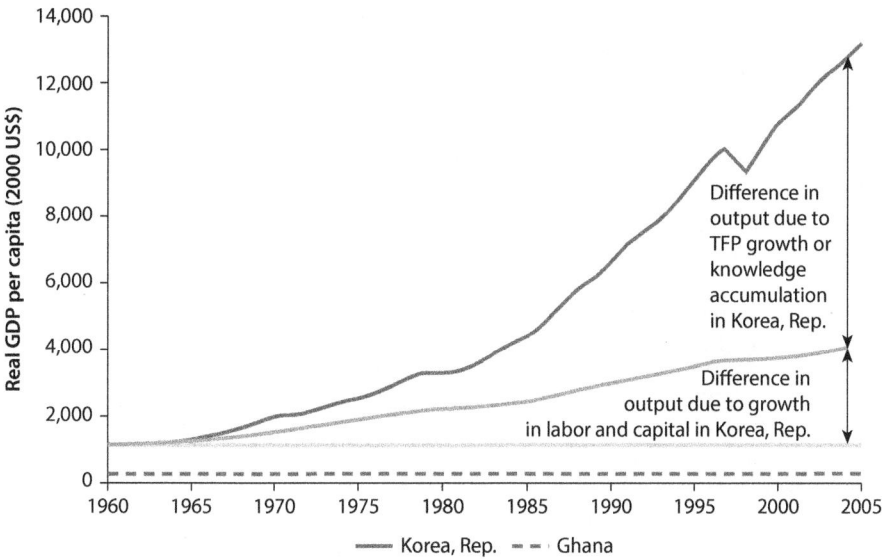

Source: World Bank 2010.
Note: GDP = gross domestic product; TFP = total factor productivity.

Table 4.3 Conventional Breakdown of Sources of Growth, 1970–2000

Indicator	Average annual growth of GDP per worker	Average annual growth of capital-labor ratio	Average annual growth of total factor productivity
Low income	0.17	0.25	−0.07
Lower-middle income	1.01	0.61	0.40
Upper-middle income	0.99	0.59	0.40
New tigers	3.79	1.70	2.09
Old tigers	4.89	2.37	2.52
High income	1.95	1.00	0.95

Source: Hulten and Isaksson 2007.
Note: Old tigers refers to Hong Kong SAR, China; the Republic of Korea; Singapore; and Taiwan, China. New tigers refers to China, India, Indonesia, Malaysia, and Thailand. GDP = gross domestic product.

attributed to innovation or the technology-related improvements pursued by Korea, with the remainder arising from the growth in capital and labor.

Looking at the World Bank classification by income group, Hulten and Isaksson (2007) noted that capital deepening appears to be more important as an explanation of growth in countries at lower levels of income, while TFP is more important for those countries that grew fastest (tiger economies; see table 4.3). Capital deepening, or the average annual growth rate in the capital-labor ratio, accounted for a greater proportion of output or the average annual growth of GDP per worker in the lower-income economies.

Furthermore, TFP has been credited with accounting for the difference in levels of development across countries. Isaksson (2007), in reviewing the literature on TFP, highlighted the factors captured in TFP. He identified these

Table 4.4 Level of Productivity in Countries of Various Incomes, 1970–2000

Indicator	Log of GDP per worker	Log of capital-labor ratio	Log of TFP
Low income	7.76	2.61	5.15
Lower-middle income	9.08	3.14	5.93
Upper-middle income	9.76	3.45	6.31
New tigers	8.09	2.78	5.31
Old tigers	9.83	3.48	6.35
High income	10.57	3.81	6.77

Source: Hulten and Isaksson 2007.
Note: Old Tigers refers to Hong Kong SAR, China; the Republic of Korea; Singapore; and Taiwan, China. *New tigers* refers to China, India, Indonesia, Malaysia, and Thailand. GDP = gross domestic product; TFP = total factor productivity.

Table 4.5 Decomposition of the Predicted Growth in National Market Shares from an Estimated Empirical Model of Cross-Country Competitiveness, 1961–73

Country	Japan	United Kingdom	United States
Growth in technological capabilities	66.9	6.9	−0.6
Rise in relative unit labor costs	−0.9	0.8	1.6
Initial technological capabilities (catch-up)	20.9	15.9	7.3
Investment as a share of GDP, and growth of world demand	16.5	−39.8	−38.2
Total growth in market share (predicted by model)	103.3	−16.2	−29.8

Source: Fagerberg 1988.
Note: GDP = gross domestic product.

factors as competition, the rule of law, enforcement of contracts, R&D, and capital accumulation. Using productivity data from countries of various incomes over the period 1970–2000, Hulten and Isaksson (2007) show that the share of TFP growth in output per worker, that is, the log of TFP, is always greater than that of capital deepening, the log of capital-labor ratio for all countries (see table 4.4).

Fagerberg (1987, 1988) suggests that innovation is one of the key factors affecting differential growth rates among countries. Table 4.5 examines the results from a model of international competitiveness that decomposes the predicted growth in national market shares into four elements for Japan, the United Kingdom, and the United States. What stands out in this table is the growth in indigenous technological capabilities in Japan, which accounts for the largest share in its competitiveness over the 1961–73 period. By contrast, the loss of world trade shares by the United Kingdom and the United States may be attributed to weak capital accumulation (investment as a share of GDP and growth of world demand) arising from the high share of military spending in these two economies.

The link between innovation and competitiveness focuses on longer-term technological competitiveness. Innovation has played and continues to play a key role in changing or transforming the way in which the world's technological systems are structured. Figure 4.3 charts the four poles around which technological systems are structured—energy, matter, life, and time—and also charts how these poles are affected by the transformations taking place in the world's technological

Figure 4.3 Major Technical Systems from the Middle Ages through the Present

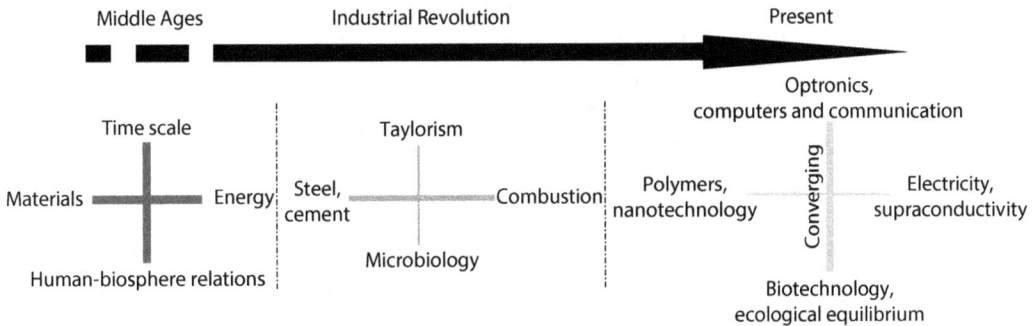

Source: World Bank 2010.

systems. Change depends on how quickly humans adapt to the new technologies. The world moved over time from the agricultural revolution in the Middle Ages through the Industrial Revolution to the "cognitive revolution" today (World Bank 2010). This cognitive revolution is taking the form of a knowledge economy characterized by rapid developments in science and technology. These developments call for new skills and higher levels of education in order to exploit the innovation potential that the advances are unearthing. Investment in this knowledge, whether through education or through R&D, is critical for economic progress and prosperity. Access to knowledge is key for innovation.

Longer-term technological competitiveness supposes that the faster growth of output and exports achieved by innovation, along with new lines of value creation, drives up the domestic currency, reflecting an increase in international competitiveness. This type of technological competitiveness, classified as neo-Schumpeterian,[11] pertains when countries (or firms) that are most successful in innovation achieve a sustainable increase in the share of world trade (or in the share of the relevant world market) and also expand the overall magnitude of world trade and the world market (Cantwell 2005). Traistaru-Siedschlag et al. (2006) identify a number of researchers who have shown that innovating firms are more likely to export and have a higher share of exports than those firms that do not engage in R&D. Traistaru-Siedschlag et al. (2006, 7) cite the work of "Kumar and Siddhartan (1994) for Indian firms, Braunerhjelm et al. (1996) for Swedish manufacturers, Nassimbeni (2001) and Basile (2001) for Italian plants, Özçelik and Taymaz (2004) in the case of Turkey." Although it remains an underresearched area, Traistaru-Siedschlag et al. (2006) note other studies showing the positive effect of exporting on innovation.[12]

The Commission on Growth and Development (2008) identified 13 economies worldwide that had achieved at least 25 years of consecutive growth above 7 percent.[13] One of the five main elements identified for this successful growth pattern was their participation in the global economy and the importance of innovation and technology in their economic development. "To put it very simply, they imported what the rest of the world knew, and exported what it wanted" (Commission on Growth and Development 2008, 22).

The ability of an economy to innovate by upgrading and restructuring its industries based on learning from foreign technologies has focused attention on the firm and the industry. The scope for interaction between the firm and the industry feeds into the competitiveness of the local area, the region, and the nation. The scope for interaction between the firm and its location has concentrated the research effort along two similar paths. At one level, the research has focused on the geography of this interaction, and academic attention has concentrated on "innovative regions and milieux," "high-tech areas," "clusters of knowledge based industries," and "knowledge spillovers."[14] At a second and complementary level, the research reflects the fact that innovation requires a range of complementary activities that include organizational changes, training, testing, and marketing. It also takes into consideration the fact that innovation is a highly collaborative endeavor requiring input from many participants and thus best undertaken where these stakeholders converge. Here the academic and policy work has adopted a "system of innovation"[15]approach that concentrates on the entire process of innovation rather than just one element, such as the supply of technology. The innovation system approach informs policy for innovation, as discussed in the following sections.

Policies for Innovation

A new global context heralds an unprecedented role for innovation. The following section will examine both the role for innovation in the wake of the 2008 financial crisis and its role in meeting the economic and social challenges of the modern age against the background of increasing global interdependence. The share of world merchandise trade to world GDP increased from 32 percent in 1990 to 51 percent in 2011, while trade in services increased from 7.5 percent of GDP in 1990 to 11.4 percent in 2011.[16] Figure 4.4 shows that cross-border capital flows increased from less than $1 trillion in 1990 to $11 trillion in 2007. Furthermore, FDI inward stock as a percentage of GDP increased from 9.6 percent in 1990 to 30.3 percent in 2010. These global developments provide a rich context for the development of policy to promote innovation.

The legacy of the 2008 financial crisis was manifest in the weak and sluggish recovery in the developed economies, in contrast with the stronger growth in the emerging markets (see figure 4.5). Recovery from the recent financial crisis depends upon new sources of economic growth. Many of the traditional sources of growth are declining in importance. Stagnating populations in the developed economies have implications for labor inputs in long-run economic growth, while physical capital inputs face diminishing returns and may be insufficient to strengthen long-term growth (OECD 2010). Technology can be a means of buttressing growth and achieving sustainable growth over the longer term. Developed economies work at or near the technology frontier, and developing economies have the potential to catch up by acquiring existing knowledge. Most of this knowledge is already in the public domain and can be acquired through formal modes as well as through informal channels such as copying and reverse

Figure 4.4 Cross-Border Capital Inflows, 1985–2009

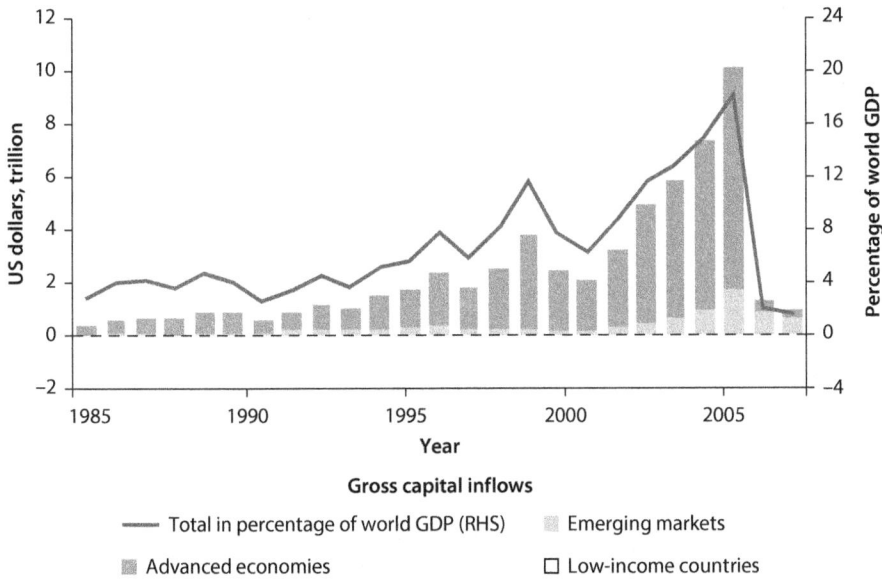

Gross capital inflows

— Total in percentage of world GDP (RHS)   ▦ Emerging markets

▦ Advanced economies   ☐ Low-income countries

Source: IMF 2010.
Note: GDP = gross domestic product.

engineering. The success of these efforts depends upon the developing economy having its own capabilities to acquire, use, and create knowledge. There is a clear role for policy in meeting these challenges.

Innovation provides the foundation for new industries, businesses, and jobs by improving competitiveness and economic growth. It is already an important contributor to growth in some countries. Figure 4.6 shows the contribution made to labor productivity growth by innovation. First, investment in intangible assets, that is, investment in R&D, software, databases, and skills, accounts for just as much as investment in physical capital in the majority of countries. Investment in intangible assets and multifactor productivity (MFP) accounted for between two-thirds and three-quarters of labor productivity growth between 1995 and 2006 in Austria, Finland, Sweden, the United Kingdom, and the United States.

Market failure, or indeed the absence of markets, acts as a constraint on the development of innovations. There is increasing pressure to deal with the various social challenges such as climate change, health, food security, and access to water. These challenges are global in nature and cannot be dealt with by one single country. The challenges require commitment and coordination at an international level. The pricing of externalities, such as carbon emissions, is an important catalyst for innovation. Tax policies can also help by providing a signal and fostering a market for innovation. Removing subsidies for environmentally harmful substances can also help (OECD 2010).

The distribution and use of existing technologies are key for economic and social challenges. They are particularly important for developing economies, where simple technologies can significantly increase welfare. World Bank (2010)

Figure 4.5 Global Growth in Real GDP, 2000–12 (quarterly change from prior year)

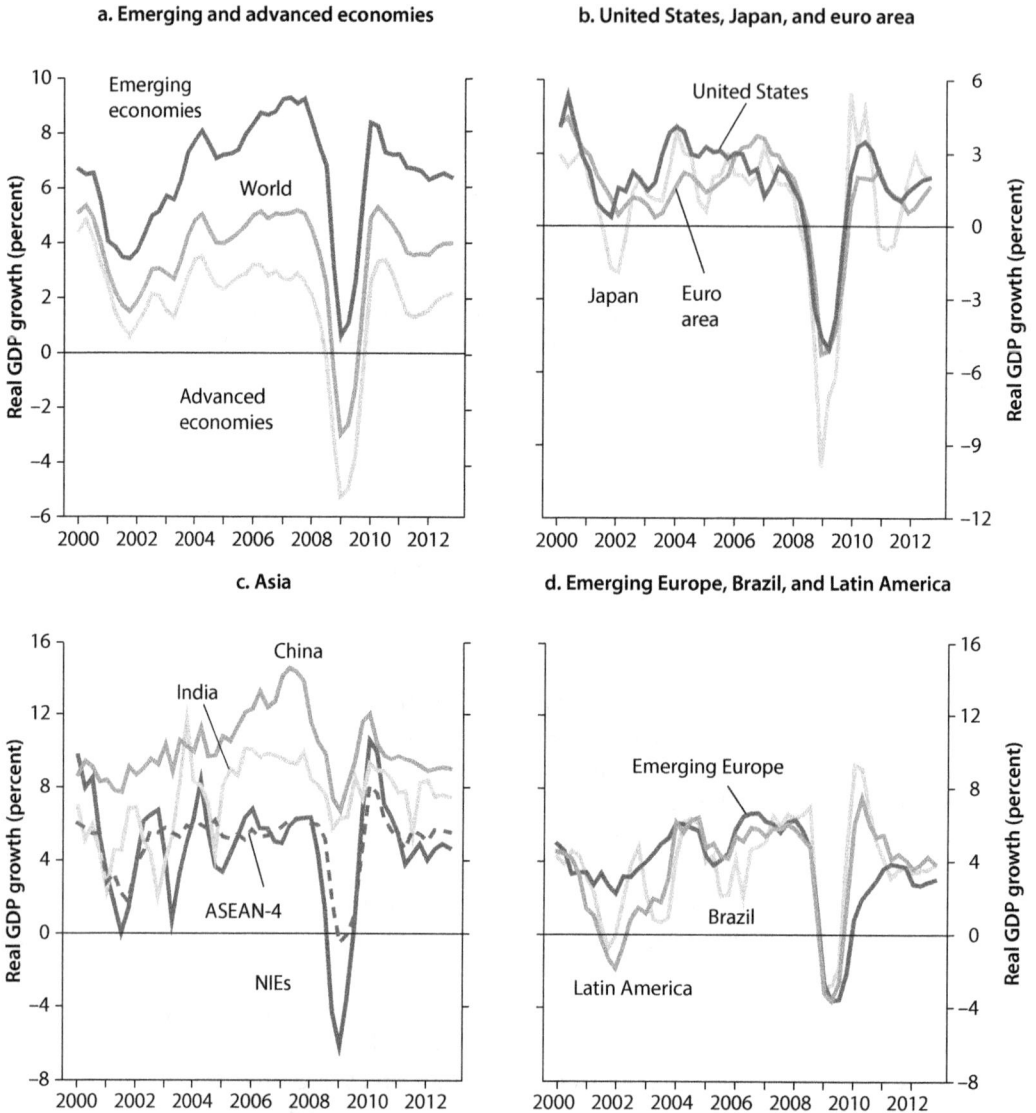

a. Emerging and advanced economies

b. United States, Japan, and euro area

c. Asia

d. Emerging Europe, Brazil, and Latin America

Source: IMF 2011.

Note: IMF = International Monetary Fund; ASEAN = Association of Southeast Asian Nations; NIEs = newly industrialized economies. In panel a, emerging economies are Argentina, Brazil, Bulgaria, Chile, China, Colombia, Hungary, India, Indonesia, Latvia, Lithuania, Malaysia, Mexico, Peru, Philippines, Poland, Russian Federation, South Africa, Thailand, Turkey, and Venezuela, RB; advanced economies are those that report quarterly data—Australia; Canada; Czech Republic; Denmark; Euro area; Hong Kong SAR, China; Israel; Japan; Korea, Rep.; New Zealand; Norway; Singapore; Sweden; Switzerland; Taiwan, China. In panel c, ASEAN countries are Indonesia, Malaysia, Philippines, and Thailand. In panel d, emerging European countries are Bulgaria, Hungary, Latvia, Lithuania, and Poland; Latin American countries are Argentina, Brazil, Chile, Colombia, Mexico, Peru, and Venezuela, RB.

Figure 4.6 Innovation Accounts for a Large Share of Labor Productivity Growth, Percentage Contributions, 1995–2006

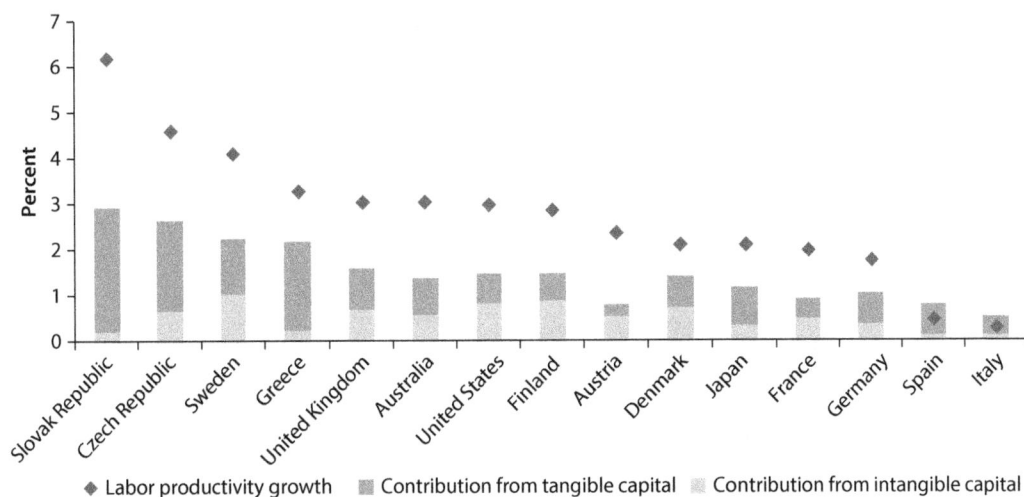

♦ Labor productivity growth ▓ Contribution from tangible capital ▒ Contribution from intangible capital

Source: Wyckoff 2010.

Table 4.6 Percentage of Rural and Urban Population with Access to Clean Water, 1990 and 2004

Location	Total		Rural		Urban	
	1990	2004	1990	2004	1990	2004
Region						
East Asia and Pacific	71.8	78.5	61.4	69.8	97.3	91.9
Europe and Central Asia	91.7	91.7	83.4	79.8	97.0	98.7
Latin America and the Caribbean	82.8	91.0	50.0	73.0	92.6	96.0
Middle East and North Africa	87.5	89.5	78.9	80.8	96.1	96.3
South Asia	70.6	64.4	64.9	81.3	88.6	93.6
Sub-Saharan Africa	48.9	56.2	36.1	42.4	81.9	80.1
World	76.4	82.7	63.2	72.2	95.2	94.5
Countries						
High income	99.8	99.5	99.1	98.5	99.8	99.8
Low and middle income	72.1	79.9	60.6	70.5	93.3	92.8
Low income	64.3	75.0	56.7	69.4	87.0	88.1

Source: World Bank 2010.

highlights three areas in which existing technology can improve welfare—vaccines, access to water, and sanitation. Table 4.6 shows the percentage of rural and urban population with access to clean water in 1990 and 2004. The technology to provide clean water is relatively simple and has benefitted from improvements in the past decade, but roughly 20 percent of the population of low- and middle-income countries continue to lack access to clean water. The disparity is even more pronounced between rural and urban dwellers—roughly 30 percent of rural dwellers do not have access to clean water, compared to 7 percent of urban dwellers.

Clusters of Competitiveness • http://dx.doi.org/10.1596/978-1-4648-0049-8

Table 4.7 Pace of Dissemination of Major Technologies, 1748–2000

Technology	Period in which technology was initially discovered				Number
	1748–1900	1900–50	1950–75	1975–2000	
Transportation					21
Shipping (steam)	83				57
Shipping (steam motor)	180				93
Rail (passenger)	126				99
Rail (freight)	124				153
Vehicle (private)	96				123
Vehicle (commercial)	63				109
Aviation (passenger)		60			103
Aviation (freight)		60			
Communications					
Telegram	91				77
Telephone	99				156
Radio		69			154
Television		59			156
Cable TV		50			98
Personal computer			24		134
Internet use			23		151
Mobile phone				16	150
Manufacturing					
Spindle (ring)	111				50
Steel (OHF)	125				50
Electrification	78				155
Steel (EAF)		92			91
Synthetic textiles		36			75
Medical (OECD only)					
Cataract surgery	251				19
X-ray		93			27
Dialysis		33			29
Mammography			33		18
Liver transplant			28		29
Heart transplant			28		27
CAT scan			18		29
Lithotripter				15	26
Average (excluding medical)	106.9	60.9	23.5	16.0	
Average (including medical)	118.9	61.3	25.7	15.5	

Source: World Bank 2010.
Note: The table indicates the number of years elapsed between the time the technology was invented and the time it had reached 80 percent of reporting countries. CAT = computer-assisted tomography; EAF = electric arc furnace; OECD = Organisation for Economic Co-operation and Development; OHF = open hearth furnace.

Table 4.7 examines the speed at which major global technologies were implemented. Two key trends emerge. First, the speed at which the major technologies were disseminated over countries has increased over time. For example, for over 80 percent of the countries surveyed, key innovations developed between 1748 and 1900 took slightly more than 100 years on average to disseminate; those developed between 1900 and 1950 took an average of 61 years; those between 1950 and 1975 took an average of 24 years; and those between 1970 and 2000 took an average of 16 years (World Bank 2010).

The speed at which innovations are being adapted has increased over time. The importance and rate of adaptation of innovations and inventions are the subjects of recent literature that examines the extent to which innovation and new technology are driving economic growth.[17]

The second trend is that while there has been improvement in the distribution of technology to the capital and major cities of developing countries, the rate of dissemination within these countries is slow (World Bank 2010). This was evident from table 4.6, which showed that the rate of rural access to clean water was markedly different from the urban access rate. Of concern is that access to basic technologies such as electricity and paved roads also remains outside of the reach of many.

How Can Government Help?

The discussion so far has highlighted a broad view of innovation that argues for well-specified policies across a range of areas. Innovation depends on a favorable economic environment that encompasses education, governance, and infrastructure. These areas may be problematic for developing countries, "but experience shows not only that proactive innovation policies are possible and effective but also that they help create an environment for broader reforms" (World Bank 2010, 2). Government has a key role to play. Governments bring about the regulations and markets that enable firms to innovate. They can launch programs in education and training, in product and labor markets, in public research institutions, and in policies for networking and knowledge exchange between firms and markets. "Pro-growth tax reforms can also help to strengthen growth and innovation" (OECD 2010, 2).

Government plays both a direct and an indirect role when it comes to fostering innovation. For example, in the area of technology promotion, government can play a direct role through supporting innovative efforts for space exploration or defense. Indirectly, government can create a favorable climate for innovation through enactment of supporting laws. Macroeconomic, business, and governance conditions all determine the capabilities for innovation in each country. At the same time, each country will have its own needs for innovation. Policy changes in these areas can bridge the gap between capabilities and needs. Moreover, specific innovation policy of and by itself can be an important trigger for change in areas that may be lacking.

Figure 4.7 presents the various factors that influence a developing country's capabilities in innovation. Developed countries are assumed to be at the technological frontier and through various links—trade, FDI, and diaspora and other networks—affect positively the capacity for innovation in the developing countries. These transmission channels can be enhanced by policies to create competencies and build an innovation-friendly business climate. These policies

Figure 4.7 Determinants of Technology Upgrading in Developing Countries

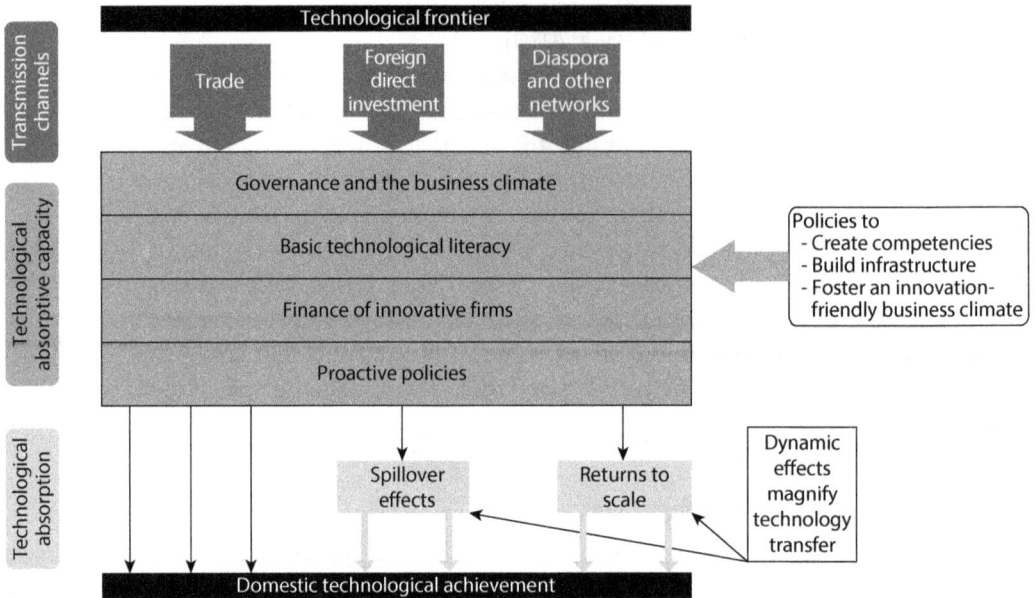

Source: World Bank 2010.

target the technological absorptive capacity of the developing economy, and through spillover effects and returns to scale they result in technology transfer that increases domestic technological achievement in the developing economy.

Figure 4.7 illustrates the involvement of both the private and public sector in what the World Bank (2010, 8) has termed the "innovation system." In this system, public and private organizations work together to foster the technological, commercial, and financial competencies and inputs required for innovation. The government can facilitate the innovation system in a number of ways:

- supporting innovators through appropriate incentives and mechanisms;
- removing obstacles to innovative initiatives;
- establishing responsive research structures; and
- forming a creative and receptive population through appropriate educational systems (World Bank 2010, 8).

The World Bank (2010) illustrates the role of the government in promoting innovation in figure 4.8. Innovation policy requires input from many different areas, including education, trade, investment, decentralization, and finance. The approach suggests a holistic role for government involving many departments in order to achieve a "fundamentally horizontal and interdepartmental innovation policy" (World Bank 2010, 9). Moreover, subnational governments have a key role to play, as innovation takes place in firms and enterprises at the local level.

Figure 4.8 Growing Innovation: The Government as Gardener

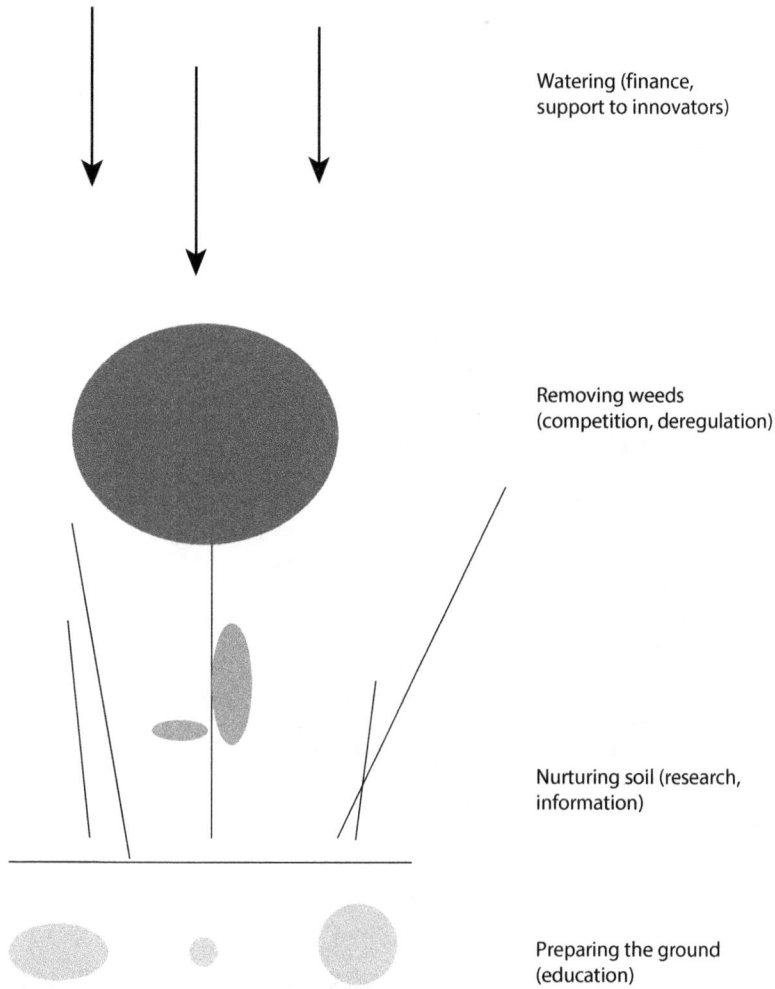

Watering (finance,
support to innovators)

Removing weeds
(competition, deregulation)

Nurturing soil (research,
information)

Preparing the ground
(education)

Source: World Bank 2010.

The OECD (2010) proposes a similar innovation strategy that is built upon five priorities for government:

- empowering people to innovate;
- unleashing innovation in firms;
- creating and applying knowledge;
- applying innovation to address global and social challenges;
- improving the governance and measurement of policies for innovation.

The principles underlying these priorities are shown in table 4.8, where we also include the strategies under the "gardening" approach suggested by the World Bank (2010).

Clusters of Competitiveness • http://dx.doi.org/10.1596/978-1-4648-0049-8

Table 4.8 OECD and World Bank Policy Principles for Innovation

OECD		World Bank	
Priority	*Principles*	*Priority*	*Principles*
Empowering people to innovate	Education Training Knowledge transmission	Preparing the ground	Education
Unleashing innovation in firms	Foster entrepreneurship Enhance access to finance Build foundations for innovation with sound framework conditions Foster markets for innovative goods, services, and processes	Removing weeds	Competition Deregulation
Creating and applying knowledge	Foster strong and effective public research Invest in a knowledge-supporting infrastructure Foster efficient knowledge flows, networks, and markets Unleash innovation in the public sector	Nurturing soil	Research Information
Applying innovation to address global and social challenges	Foster international cooperation Tackle key challenges through innovation: climate change, health, and food security Bridge the gap in economic development through innovation	Watering	Finance Support to innovators
Improving the governance and measurement of policies for innovation	Link science, technology, and innovation policies to economic growth Develop data infrastructure to measure the determinants and impact of innovation Account for the role of innovation in public sector Promote new statistical methods and interdisciplinary approaches to data collection Promote measurement of innovation for social goals and social impacts of innovation		

Source: OECD 2010; World Bank 2010.
Note: OECD = Organisation for Economic Co-operation and Development.

The elements of innovation policy discussed by recent OECD and the World Bank publications on innovation strategy—and encapsulated in table 4.8—suggest a "whole of government" approach encompassing cross-department cooperation and extending to local and regional as well as national governments. The differing country contexts in terms of needs and capabilities suggest the fallacy of a one-size-fits-all policy. Indeed, the World Bank (2010, 48) notes that "innovation agendas in the developed and in the developing world will differ significantly."[18] The economic, cultural, and social settings particular to each country suggest a need to understand the "specific motivations and behavior as people innovate, create new things, adapt their institutions, and manage their businesses" (World Bank 2010, 69). Berdegué (2005) and Gupta (2007) stress the importance of aligning innovation policies with social settings.

Empowering People to Innovate or Preparing the Ground
Both education and training systems are key when it comes to "empowering people to innovate" or "preparing the ground." The OECD argues for flexible

systems of education and training that provide people with the foundation for learning and developing broad ranges of skills and that make it possible for them to upgrade their skills and adapt to changing market conditions. The OECD study identifies universities and vocational training colleges as "essential nodes in the innovation system," which produce students with the capacity for lifelong learning as well as being the "anchor for clusters of innovative activity" (OECD 2010, 10). On-the-job training has an important role to play in lifelong learning. It is particularly relevant in developing economies, where it is responsible for "more skills development than all other types of training combined" (World Bank 2010, 16). Skills such as "critical thinking, creativity, communication, user orientation and team work in addition to domain-specific and linguistic skills" are identified by the OECD study as being critical for innovation (OECD 2010, 9).

The World Bank study calls for skills development in the informal economy, "which can represent 30 percent or more of nonfarm employment in a number of developing economies" (World Bank 2010, 16). Vocational training colleges should work more closely with businesses through engaging workers and employers in curriculum development. Entrepreneurship education should be part of the curriculum, and female participation in science and technology subjects should be encouraged. Labor market policy should provide incentives for women to enter the workplace, such as availability of child care and tax and benefit systems, and should support workplace practices that favor women's participation in the labor market (OECD 2010). Investing in a well-educated workforce may be a double-edged sword for developing economies, since it poses the risk of a brain drain. Therefore, policy in these economies should strive for a "brain circulation" that would connect talented migrants with their home country as "creators of enterprises, openers of new markets, sources of venture capital, or facilitators of institutional reforms" (World Bank 2010, 17).

Unleashing Innovation or Removing the Weeds

"Unleashing innovations" or "removing the weeds" calls for policies that will put in place framework conditions to support competition that fosters innovation. Under this rubric, policies would aim to mobilize funding for firms through well-functioning financial markets and ease the access to finance for new firms. In addition, policies would aim to foster open markets and competitive markets predicated on healthy risk taking and creative activity. Policies would focus on entrepreneurship and on small- and medium-size firms, particularly new firms. The World Bank study notes that many areas of government will be involved in establishing framework conditions. These tasks are "particularly necessary, but difficult, in developing country contexts" (World Bank 2010, 13).

Well-functioning financial markets, which provide access to finance for new and small innovative firms with the necessary early-stage financing and networks for business angels and venture capital, are critical for promoting innovation and a prime area for policy. Access to finance can be a constraint for many firms, particularly for the innovative firm that may require a long-term horizon.

Seed capital and start-up capital by business angel funds provide more than just financing; they also offer advice and experience. Government can encourage networks of business angels. Government can play a further role in ensuring that "information on intellectual assets is consistent and comparable over time and across companies" (OECD 2010, 13). This step will help investors to make better decisions about investment opportunities.

Building sound framework conditions targets the overall environment for business creation and development and has become increasingly important in the global environment. Stable macroeconomic policies help to reduce uncertainty. Innovation would also benefit from open international markets that facilitated the exchange and spread of knowledge. Government policies can help speed up the knowledge-adoption process by removing tariffs or other restrictions on acquiring global knowledge. It could subsidize early adopters of innovation and provide support services by launching information and publicity campaigns and provide demonstration and extension services. Furthermore, it could introduce regulations requiring adoption of global innovation in certain areas, for example reducing pollution or carbon use. Finally, it could invest in human capital in order to improve the absorption capacity for new technologies. Microeconomic policies help foster open and competitive markets that are critical for innovation. Taxation policies affect investment decisions at the household and firm level and can thus affect innovation.

Policies to foster entrepreneurship may take a variety of forms that target areas of difficulty for entrepreneurs. For example, policies may focus upon reducing barriers to firm entry and exit. New firms or young firms are critical for innovation, bringing new ideas to market and taking advantage of existing technology or other opportunities that may have been neglected by older, more established firms. OECD (2010) stresses the importance of new firms for bringing new ideas to markets, as illustrated by their patent filings (see figure 4.9).

Figure 4.9 Patenting Activity of Young Firms, 2005–07

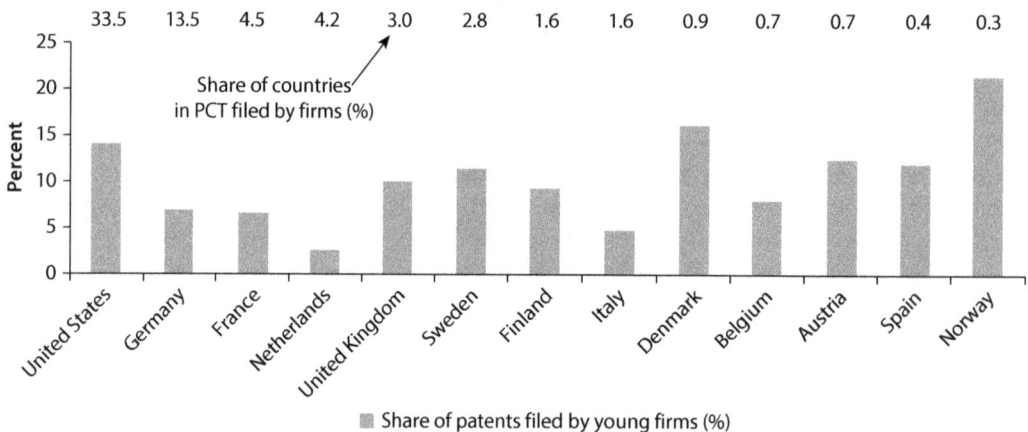

■ Share of patents filed by young firms (%)

Source: OECD 2010.
Note: Young firms are those under five years old. Data are for Patent Cooperation Treaty patents. OECD = Organisation for Economic Co-operation and Development; PCT = Patent Cooperation Treaty.

Policy may also focus on the tax system, another area that entrepreneurs identify as adversely affecting their decision to become self-employed. Policies may target a more neutral tax treatment and thus help to foster entrepreneurship. The high rate of failure endemic to new enterprises need not be such a bad thing in an environment that efficiently allows for the reallocation of resources from declining to innovative firms. Policies should foster open and competitive markets. The World Bank's *Doing Business* surveys can identify obstacles to innovation.

Governments have a role to play in fostering markets for innovation. OECD (2010, 15) identifies the following three areas in which government can play an active role: "getting prices right; opening markets for competition; and devising innovation-inducing standards and regulations."

Creating and Applying Knowledge or Nurturing the Soil

The third priority identified by the OECD, and one that loosely coincides with the World Bank's innovation strategy of "nurturing the soil," is creating and applying knowledge. Policies here would target knowledge development, sharing, and transmission from the creation and governance of public research institutes to the fostering of networks and markets that enable knowledge sharing and diffusion. Also under this priority are policies targeted at establishing an effective system of intellectual property rights and those that ensure coherence among multilevel sources of funding for R&D. In addition, policies should promote innovation in the public sector to bring about an enhancement of public service delivery and an improvement in efficiency.

The World Bank (2010) advocates that developing countries invest in their own capability to acquire, use, and create knowledge. Developing countries can dramatically improve their position by acquiring existing knowledge. Most of this knowledge is in the public domain already. Other knowledge can be acquired through formal means, and some may be acquired through informal copying and reverse engineering. The latter is the most important source of technological catch up, especially in the case of rapidly growing economies such as the United States in the 1800s; Japan, Korea, and Taiwan, China, in the 1900s; and China and India now.

Applying Knowledge to Address Global and Social Challenges or Watering the Soil

Applying innovation to address global and social challenges is another area for policy. Under this heading, we include challenges from climate change, global health, and food security. Market failure or the absence of a market for many of these challenges suggests a role for policy in helping to achieve sustainable solutions. Moreover, the scale and scope of these challenges indicates a role for government involvement at an international level.

"Proven co-operation strategies include joint investment in basic and pre-competitive research; mapping of R&D needs; technology transfer initiatives;

and scholarships and fellowships for international researchers and students" (OECD 2010, 20). An example of a multilateral effort is the United Nations Clean Development Mechanism (CDM). Academic partnerships—cross-country teaming of higher education establishments in science and technology—also facilitate technology transfer with implications for local innovation systems (OECD 2010). The solutions to meet global challenges are long term in nature and thus call for policy that is predictable and provides long-term incentives. Policies should promote private sector involvement by being flexible, and they should focus, where possible, on direct solutions to global problems. For example, "in addressing climate change, a tax on carbon will be more effective for inducing an optimal innovation path than a tax on fuel or electricity use" (OECD 2010, 22).

Innovation can play a significant role in bridging the gap in economic development at the developing economy level. Poor framework conditions and low social and human capital in developing economies present a challenge for innovation. The domestic economy needs to be very good at tapping global knowledge through all its forms—trade, technology, licensing, FDI, and participation in global value chains; foreign education and training; participation in trade fairs; global research networks, technical publications and databases; and copying and reverse engineering. Using catch-up strategies is easier than pushing back the global frontier, so the domestic economy must exploit these catch-up opportunities.

Finally, the domestic economy needs to build up its capability not just for education in general but also for entrepreneurship, business management, and science and engineering. It also requires institutions and mechanisms capable of providing re-skilling and up-skilling to keep abreast of new technology and business needs.

Improving the Governance and Measurement of Policies for Innovation

Finally, policy coherence, good governance of policies, and an improved measurement framework for innovation are essential in developing innovation policies. A "whole of government" approach is needed that includes medium- and long-term policies overseen by high-level officials at the local, regional, national, and international levels. Cooperation across government departments and complementary policies are necessary to foster an environment in which innovation can flourish. Implementing the right framework conditions will have positive spin-off benefits for the coordination of policies at the regional and local level. Improving measures of innovation is critical for policy making. The OECD (2010, 24) notes that the "current innovation indicators are too focused on the inputs of the innovation process rather than on its outcomes." It puts forward a wide range of innovation indicators for policy making and suggests that this approach be taken up at the national and international level.

Table 4.9 summarizes the elements of policy for innovation and highlights individual policy instruments that may be adopted.

Table 4.9 Summary of Innovation Policy Elements

Priority	Principles	Instruments
Empowering people to innovate	Provide education and training Foster knowledge transmission	*Education policy:* Change curriculum and pedagogy; evaluate teachers on ongoing basis; engage employers and workers in curriculum development; ensure independence, competition, excellence, entrepreneurial spirit, and flexibility in universities; provide entrepreneurial education. *Labor market policy:* End nontransparent hiring and promotion in scientific institutions; open labor markets to foreign students; ensure tax regime does not penalize mobile skilled workers.
Unleashing innovation in firms	Foster entrepreneurship Enhance access to finance Build foundations for innovation with sound framework conditions Foster markets for innovative goods, services, and processes	*Labor market policies:* Simplify and reduce start-up regulations and administrative burdens; foster open and competitive markets to facilitate the reallocation of resources that occurs when firms fail and new firms emerge. *Finance policies:* Amend bankruptcy laws to facilitate restructuring of businesses, paying attention to risk management and moral hazard. Adapt changes to develop a more neutral tax policy. Lower regulatory barriers so high–growth firms do not spend needed capital on bureaucracy; restore the health of the financial sector; develop well-functioning venture capital markets; securitize innovation-related assets (intellectual property); ease new and small firms' access to debt finance and equity finance, e.g., through risk-sharing schemes with the private sector; develop seed capital and start-up financing by business angel funds and networks. *Macroeconomic policies:* Ensure sound policies for the macroeconomy; promote openness to trade (reduce tariff barriers, dismantle nontariff barriers, and liberalize capital markets); conclude the WTO's Doha Development Agenda; promote investment, fiscal discipline, and strong and stable output growth. *Microeconomic policies:* Develop policies for competition;[a] tax policies, framework for intellectual property rights. Get prices right; develop standards and regulations governing public procurement, which provides important signals on future demand to the private sector.

table continues next page

Table 4.9 Summary of Innovation Policy Elements *(continued)*

Priority	Principles	Instruments
Creating and applying knowledge	Foster strong and effective public research Invest in a knowledge-supporting infrastructure Foster efficient knowledge flows, networks, and markets Unleash innovation in the public sector	*Microeconomic policies:* Create a strong and effective public research system; finance public research to better facilitate funding of multidisciplinary research; tie part of funding to societal objectives; recognize that private investment may not take place when time horizon is long and outputs are not immediately marketable. *Education policies:* Grant greater autonomy to universities and public research organizations; establish guidelines for collaborative arrangements between universities and public laboratories; establish criteria for evaluating research performance; attract well-trained technology transfer personnel. *Technology policies:* Promote development of ICT; adopt the new standard for Internet protocol (IPv6); promote the relationship between broadband networks and energy, health, transport, and education; foster the integration of ICT investments in physical infrastructure such as buildings, roads, transport systems, health facilities, and electricity grids; protect intellectual property rights. Promote knowledge transfer across borders through tax treaties; review cross-country differences in regulations and commercial law. Develop knowledge networking infrastructure.[b] *Competition policies:* Ensure that the patent system is not used anticompetitively.

table continues next page

Table 4.9 Summary of Innovation Policy Elements (continued)

Priority	Principles	Instruments
Applying innovation to address global and social challenges	Foster international cooperation Tackle key challenges—climate change, health, and food security—through innovation Bridge the gap in economic development through innovation	*Technology policies*[c]: Develop a new model for the governance of multilateral cooperation on international science, technology, and innovation, one focusing on the "setting of work priorities, funding and institutional arrangements to support that work," and on "procedures to ensure access to knowledge, transfer of technology and capacity building" (OECD 2010, 20). *Macroeconomic policies*: Remove trade barriers that limit technology transfer across borders and develop mechanisms that enhance technology transfer and the development of knowledge markets;[d] strengthen framework conditions in developing countries—education, basic infrastructure (transport, rural energy, irrigation); modernize agriculture, carry out poverty reduction, develop ICT, strengthen institutions. *Education policies*: Foster academic partnerships, cross-border higher education, and scientific cooperation. *Finance policies*: Develop new financing mechanisms to provide incentives for innovation, e.g., venture capital, public-private partnerships *Microeconomic policies*: Develop pricing policies for environmental externalities; develop tax policies; implement standards; make use of subsidies.
Improving the governance and measurement of policies for innovation	Link science, technology, and innovation policies to economic growth Develop data infrastructure to measure the determinants and impact of innovation Account for the role of innovation in the public sector Promote new statistical methods and interdisciplinary approaches to data collection Promote measurement of innovation for social goals and social impacts of innovation	"A whole-of-government approach to policies for innovation is needed to encourage innovation in its many forms. It requires stable platforms for coordinating actions, policies with a medium- and long-term perspective, and attention from policy makers at the highest level. It also calls for coherence and complementarities between the local, regional, national and international levels" (OECD 2010, 23).

Source: OECD 2010.

Note: WTO = World Trade Organization; ICTs = information and communication technologies; OECD = Organisation for Economic Co-operation and Development.

a. The OECD has developed a Competition Assessment Toolkit to help governments. See http//www.oecd.org/daf/competition/competitionassessmenttoolkit.htm.

b. "Some good practice exists (for example, in networking R&D [research and development] for emerging infectious diseases) but significant scale-up is required." OECD 2010, 19.

c. OECD 2010, 20.

d. For example: "voluntary patent pools and other collaborative mechanisms for reducing transaction costs to access intellectual property." OECD 2010, 20.

Conclusion

The chapter discussed the definition and measurement of innovation and high-lighted examples of the positive relationship between innovation, economic growth, and competitiveness. It then examined the elements of an effective innovation policy capable of meeting the economic and social challenges of the modern age.

The concept of innovation has evolved from a fairly narrow definition emphasizing new products and processes to a broader systemic definition that emphasizes the flow of technology and knowledge among people, enterprises, and institutions. The expanded definition calls for a more detailed measurement rubric in addition to the traditional focus on R&D spending alone. The expanding use of innovation surveys assists in providing both input and output measures of innovation, although these surveys are not yet widely used.

Innovation is necessary for growth, both for developed economies seeking to push the technology frontier further and for developing countries wanting to catch up. The literature examining the relation of innovation to growth and competitiveness illustrates innovation's significant contribution, while developments in new growth theory have enabled innovation to feature as a key explanatory variable in the endogenous growth models. Harnessing innovation for growth and competitiveness is critical in the modern, knowledge economy, particularly one recovering from recession and facing global challenges.

Unsurprisingly, a system of innovation, associated with today's economy, requires a "system of government" policy, or a "whole of government" approach. This includes coordinated demand- and supply-side policies at the local, national, and international level. There is no one-size-fits-all set of policies; the policies adapted will depend on the needs and capabilities of the underlying economies. Developing countries can learn from others but should also develop the capability to do some frontier work by investing in R&D and joining global research networks in, for example, nanotechnology and biotechnology. This step paves the way toward adapting potentially new and exciting technologies that may be key to new technological revolutions. Deciding how much to invest and in what areas depends of course on the underlying capabilities and ambitions of the country, and it also depends upon the strength of the country's entrepreneurship. Governments have a key role to play in getting innovation out of the universities and research labs and into production and use. Pursuing competitiveness through innovation is an increasingly important objective of policy, given the preeminent role of innovation in the modern, knowledge-driven economy.

Notes

1. "The 'death of distance' opens opportunities: new markets and narrower forms of specialization in 'fragmented' production and global value chains." (S. Lall n.d.)
2. Organisation for Economic Co-operation and Development (OECD 2009) notes the shortcomings of research and development (R&D) as a measure of innovation, citing its focus on inputs, technological doings, and manufacturing activity. Patent data have

also been used as measures of innovation "but they cannot measure the full extent of innovative activities and suffer from some well-known limitations" (OECD 2009, 12).

3. The Oslo Manual was developed by the OECD in 1992 "to harmonise and ensure the quality of innovation surveys" (OECD 2009, 12).

4. Cross-country comparisons, however, "should be undertaken with caution given that there are differences in both response rates and in the methods used by countries to adjust for non-responses" (OECD 2009, 29).

5. Five indicators comprise the composite indicator for output-based innovation modes. (1) New-to-market international innovators collect data on enterprises that have introduced a product or process new to international markets or have developed a new product or process in house. (2) New-to-market domestic innovators collect data on those enterprises that have introduced product innovations new to domestic markets; innovations are partly developed in house. (3) International modifiers represent those enterprises that have some in-house development activities but whose product and/or process innovations already exist on international markets. These may or may not be new to domestic markets. (4) Domestic modifiers refer to those innovating enterprises that operate only on domestic markets. Product or process innovations already exist on the domestic market but are new to the innovating enterprise. (5) Adopters are those enterprises that adopt the innovation of others (OECD 2009).

6. Inventive activities or formal innovations are measured by in-house R&D or a patent application. Collaboration is captured by the degree to which enterprises' innovations were developed with or solely by others or the level of cooperation on innovations (OECD 2009).

7. Enterprises are classified according to four groups. (1) Technological innovators engaging in product and/or process innovation only. (2) Nontechnological innovators engaging in marketing and/or organizational innovation only. (3) Technological and nontechnological innovators. (4) No innovations implemented (OECD 2009).

8. "An analysis of dual innovators can help provide a picture of how prevalent service innovation is in manufacturing enterprises (and conversely, the prevalence of goods innovation in the services sector)" (OECD 2009, 40).

9. Cited in Cantwell (2005).

10. Total factor productivity (TFP) is the growth in output that does not come from the growth in inputs; it is a proxy for innovation here. TFP and multifactor productivity (MFP) are used as measures of innovation in growth regressions. Hall (2011) surveys a number of innovation indicators that establish a quantitative link between productivity growth and innovation.

11. Fagerberg (2005) identifies the Marx-Schumpeter model of innovation in which Schumpeter holds that technological competition, or competition through innovation, is the driving force of economic development. When a firm in a given sector introduces an innovative product, it will be rewarded, and other firms will seek to emulate this. The initial advantage enjoyed by the first firm will eventually be eroded, and the effects on growth caused by the innovation will slow down. Schumpeter held that imitators would also innovate and bring about a process of innovation diffusion, that is, one important innovation sets the stage for a plethora of subsequent innovations. The interdependencies between the initial and induced innovations imply that innovations and growth concentrate in certain sectors and certain geographic areas. This process of innovation underlies much of the subsequent research on industrial growth and international trade and competitiveness.

12. Specific works cited are Salomon and Shaver (2005); Salomon (2006); Criscuolo, Haskel, and Slaughter (2005); and Castellani and Zanfei (2006).

13. These were Hong Kong SAR, China; Japan; The Republic of Korea; Malta; Singapore; Taiwan, China; Botswana; Brazil; China; Indonesia; Malaysia; Oman; and Thailand.

14. This list of four research areas is given by Traistaru-Siedschlag et al. (2006) who cite key sources for each as follows: for "innovative regions and milieux," see Camagni (1991); Ratti, Bramanti, and Gordon (1997); and Crevoisier (2001). For "high-tech areas," see Keeble and Wilkinson (1999, 2000). For "clusters of knowledge based industries," see Cooke (2002). For "knowledge spillovers," see Audretsch and Feldman (1996); and Bottazzi and Peri (2003).

15. An innovation system is "a network of organizations within an economic system that are directly involved in the creation, diffusion and use of scientific and technological knowledge, as well as the organizations responsible for the coordination and support of these processes" (SciDev Net: http://www.scidev.net/en/editorials/systems-of-innovation-their-time-has-come.html).

16. Data are from the World Bank, World Development Indicators database; see http://data.worldbank.org/indicator/TG.VAL.TOTL.GD.ZS/countries/1W?display=graph (for merchandise trade) and http://data.worldbank.org/indicator/BG.GSR.NFSV.GD.ZS/countries/1W?display=graph (for trade in services).

17. *The Economist* summarizes some of the recent research that is pessimistic about innovation; see "Has the Ideas Machine Broken Down?" January 12, 2013. http://www.economist.com/news/briefing/21569381-idea-innovation-and-new-technology-have-stopped-driving-growth-getting-increasing. See also Gordon (2012).

18. "The drivers for innovation in the developed world have been centered on getting more (performance and productivity) from less (physical, financial, human capital) for more (profit, value to the shareholder). In contrast, the drivers in the developing world are to get more (performance, productivity) from less (cost) for more and more (people)." World Bank 2010, 48.

References

Audretsch, D., and M. Feldman. 1996. "Innovative Clusters and the Industry Life Cycle." *Review of Industrial Organization* 11 (2): 253–73.

Basile, R. 2001. "Export Behaviour of Italian Manufacturing Firms over the Nineties: The Role of Innovation." *Research Policy* 30: 1185–201.

Berdegué, Julio A. 2005. "Pro-Poor Innovation Systems." International Fund for Agricultural Development, Rome. http://www.ifad.org/events/gc/29/panel/e/julio.pdf.

Bottazzi, L., and G. Peri. 2003. "Innovation and Spillovers in Regions: Evidence from European Patent Data." *European Economic Review* 47 (4): 687–710.

Braunerhjelm, P., K. Ekholm, L. Grundberg, and P. Karpaty. 1996. "Swedish Multinational Corporations: Recent Trends in Foreign Activities." Working Paper 462, Research Institute of Industrial Economics, Stockholm.

Camagni, R. 1991. "Local 'Milieu,' Uncertainty and Innovation Networks: Towards a New Dynamic Theory of Economic Space." In *Innovation Networks*, edited by R. Camagni, 121–44. London: Belhaven Press.

Cantwell, J. 2005. "Innovation and Competitiveness." In *Handbook of Innovation*, edited by J. Fagerberg, D. C. Mowery, and R. R. Nelson, 543–67. Oxford: Oxford University Press.

Castellani, D., and A. Zanfei. 2006. *Multinational Firms, Innovation and Productivity.* London: E. Elgar.

Commission on Growth and Development. 2008. *The Growth Report: Strategies for Sustained Growth and Inclusive Development.* Washington, DC: World Bank.

Cooke, P. 2002. *Knowledge Economies: Clusters, Learning and Cooperative Advantage.* London: Routledge.

Crevoisier, O. 2001. "Der Ansatz des kreativen Milieus." *Zeitschrift für Wirtschaftsgeographie* 45: 246–56.

Criscuolo, C., J. E. Haskel, and M. J. Slaughter. 2005. "Global Engagement and the Innovation Activities of Firms." Working Paper 11479, National Bureau of Economic Research, Cambridge, MA.

The Economist. 2013. Has the Ideas Machine Broken Down?" January 12, 2013. http://www.economist.com/news/briefing/21569381-idea-innovation-and-new-technology-have-stopped-driving-growth-getting-increasing.

Fagerberg, J. 1987. "A Technology Gap Approach to Why Growth Rates Differ." *Research Policy* 16 (2-4): 87–99.

———. 1988. "Why Growth Rates Differ." In *Technical Change and Economic Theory,* edited by G. Dosi, C. Freeman, R. R. Nelson, G. Silverberg, and L. L. G. Soete, 432–57. London: Frances Pinter.

———. 2005. "Innovation: A Guide to the Literature." In *Oxford Handbook of Innovation,* edited by J. Fagerberg, D. C. Mowery, and R. R. Nelson, 1–27. Oxford: Oxford University Press.

Gordon, R. J. 2012. "Is US Economic Growth Over? Faltering Innovation Confronts the Six Headwinds." Policy Insight 63, Centre for Economic Policy Research, London.

Gupta, Anil K. 2007. "Towards an Inclusive Innovation Model for Sustainable Development." Paper presented at the Global Business Policy Council of A. T. Kearney, Dubai, United Arab Emirates, December 9–11. http://www.sristi.org/.../Towards%20an%20inclusive%20innovation%model%20for%20sustainable%20development.doc.

Hall, B. H. 2011. "Using Productivity Growth as an Innovation Indicator." European Commission. http://ec.europa.eu/commission_2010-2014/geoghegan-quinn/hlp/documents/20120309-hlp-productivity-innovation_en.pdf.

Hulten, C., and A. Isaksson. 2007. "Why Development Levels Differ: The Sources of Differential Economic Growth in a Panel of High and Low Income Countries." NBER Working Paper 13469, National Bureau of Economic Research, Cambridge, MA.

IMF (International Monetary Fund). 2010. "The Fund's Role Regarding Cross-Border Capital Flows." Strategy, Policy and Review Department and the Legal Department, IMF, Washington, DC. http://www.imf.org/external/np/pp/eng/2010/111510.pdf.

———. 2011. *World Economic Outlook.* Washington, DC: IMF.

Isaksson, A. 2007. "Determinants of Total Factor Productivity: A Literature Review." Geneva, Switzerland: United Nations Development Organization.

Keeble, D., and F. Wilkinson. 1999. "Collective Learning and Knowledge Development in the Evolution of Regional Clusters of High-technology SMEs in Europe." *Regional Studies* 33 (special issue): 295–303.

———, eds. 2000. *High-technology Clusters, Networking and Collective Learning in Europe.* Aldershot, UK: Ashgate.

Kumar, N., and N. S. Siddhartan. 1994. "Technology, Firm Size, and Export Behavior in Developing Countries." *Journal of Developing Studies* 31 (2): 288–309.

Lall, S. n.d. "Competitiveness, FDI, Trade and Innovation: A Global Perspective," slide presentation, Economics Department, University of Oxford. http://www.slideworld .com/slideshows.aspx/Competitiveness-FDI-trade-and-innovation-A-global-ppt-320737.

Lichtenberg, F. 1992. "R&D Investment and International Productivity Differences." Working Paper 4161, National Bureau of Economic Research, Cambridge, MA.

Nassimbeni, G. 2001. "Technology, Innovation Capacity, and the Export Attitude of Small Manufacturing Firms: A Logit/Tobit Model." *Research Policy* 30: 245–62.

Nelson, R. R., and H. Pack. 1999. "The Asian Miracle and Modern Growth Theory." *Economic Journal* 109 (457): 416–36.

OECD (Organisation for Economic Co-operation and Development). 2009. *Innovation in Firms: A Microeconomic Perspective.* Paris, France: OECD.

———. 2010. "Ministerial Report on the OECD Innovation Strategy. Innovation to Strengthen Growth and Address Global Challenges." Key Findings. May. Paris, France: OECD. http://www.oecd.org/sti/45326349.pdf.

Özçelik, E., and E. Taymaz. 2004. "Does Innovativeness Matter for International Competitiveness in Developing Countries? The Case of Turkish Manufacturing Industries." *Research Policy* 33:409–24.

Petrakos, G., P. Arvanitidis, and S. Pavleas. 2007. "Determinants of Economic Growth: The Experts' View." DYNREG Working Paper 20/2007. http://www.esri.ie/research/ research_areas/international_economics/dynreg/papers/Working_Paper_No._20.pdf.

Ratti, R., A. Bramanti, and R. Gordon, eds. 1997. *The Dynamics of Innovative Regions: The GREMI Approach.* Aldershot, UK: Ashgate.

Salomon, R. 2006. "Spillovers to Foreign Market Participants: Assessing the Impact of Export Strategies on Innovative Productivity." *Strategic Organization* 4 (2): 135–64.

Salomon, R., and J. M. Shaver. 2005. "Learning by Exporting: New Insights from Examining Firm Innovation." *Journal of Economics and Management Strategy* 14 (2): 431–60.

Traistaru-Siedschlag, I., ed., G. Murphy, M. Schiffbauer, G. Petrakos, L. Resmini, C. Pitelis, G. Maier, M. Trippl, P. Nijkamp, P. van Hemert, J. Vilrokx, A. Rodríguez-Pose, J. Damjian, and C. Kostev. 2006. "Dynamic Growth Regions, Innovation and Competitiveness in a Knowledge Based World Economy: A Survey of Theory and Empirical Literature." Workpackage No. 1, DYNREG, Economic and Social Research Institute. http://www.esri.ie/research/research_areas/international_ economics/dynreg/papers/DYNREG_D1.1.pdf.

Ulku, H. 2004. "R&D Innovation and Economic Growth: An Empirical Analysis." Working Paper WP/04/185, International Monetary Fund, Washington, DC.

World Bank. 2010. *Innovation Policy: A Guide for Developing Countries.* Washington, DC: World Bank. https://openknowledge.worldbank.org/bitstream/handle/10986/2460/5 48930PUB0EPI11C10Dislosed061312010.pdf?sequence=1.

Wyckoff, A. 2010. "OECD's Innovation Strategy: Key Findings and Policy Messages." Slide presentation, Organisation for Economic Co-operation and Development, Paris, France. http://www.oecd.org/site/innovationstrategy/45154092.ppt.

CHAPTER 5

Competitiveness and Clusters

"A cluster is a system of interconnection between private and public sector entities. It usually comprises a group of companies, suppliers, service providers, and associated institutions in a particular field, linked by externalities and complementarities" (World Bank 2009, vii). Clusters usually have a specific spatial dimension as well because interlinked firms often concentrate in a specific geographic area. First proposed by Michael Porter in 1990, cluster development has been embraced by policy makers and academics as a means for stimulating an area's economic development and growth. It has become increasingly important in the context of globalization, which has left many regions and nations struggling to remain competitive. Governments and private sector entities, acting either as a cluster initiative (CI) organization or through a cluster-based competitiveness project, support links among firms and industries at a regional level to promote an area's growth and competitiveness. Initially associated with developed economies, cluster-based competitiveness projects have since 2000 also been implemented in developing economies.

Public policy, through regional policy as well as policy for science and technology and industry, has implications for cluster development and competitiveness. The optimal form and depth of policy to promote cluster development remain subject to debate. Policy for cluster development at the regional level has focused mostly on lagging regions. Science and technology policies focus mainly on promoting growth efforts among technology companies and on supporting research and development (R&D), while industrial policies strive to promote an area's growth, perhaps by focusing on small and medium enterprises (SMEs). The different types of policies are not mutually exclusive; regional, science and technology, and industrial policies may all share the common goal of innovation, which is critical for long-term productivity growth.

The chapter examines the background to cluster development and competitiveness and then goes on to discuss some CIs and cluster-based competitiveness projects. The final section examines the policy implications of CIs.

Background to Clusters

Agglomeration or clustering occurs at many geographic levels and can take many forms. Scale externalities and knowledge spillovers promote agglomeration, which leads to different outcomes depending upon whether these spillovers operate at the general level or at the level of related firms and industries. Outcomes also depend upon whether spillovers improve static efficiency and flexibility in general or innovation and upgrading of competitiveness specifically (see table 5.1; Ketels, Lindqvist, and Sölvell 2008).

Agglomeration spillovers that arise from economic activity in general and that promote efficiency and flexibility at the urban level lead to metropolises and to industrial districts at the level of technologically related industries (table 5.1). These agglomeration effects are also referred to as economies of scale and scope. A more dynamic, global world, where firms and industries are involved in innovation and upgrading, leads to clusters that rely upon knowledge creation and innovation as well as the traditional flows of goods and services. More generally, at the level of the region, this innovation and upgrading can lead to the concept of the creative region.[1]

"Agglomerations of economic activity in general, and clusters in particular, are natural economic and social phenomena, both in earlier times and in the modern economy" (Ketels, Lindqvist, and Sölvell 2008, 3). Cortright (2006) traces clusters' theoretical background to the social sciences. He begins with the contributions from the neoclassical school of economic thought and progresses to contributions from social scientists emphasizing nonmarket social forces and relationships, such as customs/traditions, technological change, and social networks (see table 5.2).

There are many types of clusters, each with its own characteristics. Ketels, Lindqvist, and Sölvell (2008, 3) suggest that clusters differ on a number of dimensions:

• Well-established clusters versus clusters that are just emerging;
• Large and dense clusters with a multitude of related industries and associated organizations and institutions, as opposed to thinner and smaller clusters;
• Manufacturing-oriented clusters such as automotive versus more service-oriented clusters such as financial services;
• Science-driven clusters and clusters in traditional sectors;
• Clusters with strong external links and global reach (hot spots) as opposed to clusters with a mere regional reach.

Table 5.1 Four Types of Economic Agglomerations

	Economic activity in general	Technologically related industries
Efficiency (scale) and flexibility	Metropolises	Industrial districts
Innovation and upgrading	Creative regions	Clusters

Source: Ketels, Lindqvist, and Sölvell 2008.

Table 5.2 Social Science Contribution to Understanding of Clusters

	Summary	Contributors
Neoclassical		
Alfred Marshall	Marshall is credited with providing the first clear description of industry clusters. He identified 3 key reasons (labor market pooling, supplier specialization, knowledge spillovers) for why industrial clusters would emerge and in doing so identified "external economies"—productive benefits that are not captured by the individual firms that create them	Marshall (1920)
Regional science	Regional scientists refined Marshall's idea that firms benefit from being in close proximity and identified *localization economies* (gains from proximity to similar firms) and *urbanization economies* (gains from proximity to dissimilar firms); the concept of space was reintroduced into thinking about the economy; interest in the field waned after the 1960s, due in large part to its lack of a theoretical basis	Isard (1956) Hoover and Giarratani (1948) Chinitz (1961)
Jane Jacobs	Although not an economist by training, Jacobs's view that the creation and development of new products and technologies as the source of economic development occurred most successfully in cities where inhabitants cluster and generate new ideas and her broadening of urbanization economies to include other types of diversity	Jacobs (1969)
New economic geography	Rekindling of interest in Marshall's theory about why firms locate in geographic agglomerations; models indicate the geographic clusters of firms likely to form when increasing returns to scale are strong; firms have power to set prices; transportation costs are low; and customers, suppliers, and workers are geographically mobile	Fujita, Krugman, and Venables (1999)
Urban and regional economics	Economists study the spatial aspects of a variety of economic problems; debate about the relative importance of localization and urbanization economies; no consensus on whether industrial specialization or diversity is more important to regional growth	Henderson (1997) Glaeser et al. (1992)
The social and institutional tradition[a]		
Business organization	Analyzes the organization of production within and between firms. During the first half of the 20th century, the organization of production was dominated by "mass production" or Fordist production systems. Large firms could use economies of scale in production and in marketing to achieve lower costs and dominate markets	
	In several areas, groups of small firms flourished in highly specialized markets; small firms were competitive through flexible specialization; groups of firms in industrial districts were supported by a variety of institutions and culture of cooperation that enabled them to mimic or offset many of the advantages of scale economies. Termed the *second industrial divide*	Piore and Sabel (1984)
Geography and urban and regional planning	Geographers and urban and regional planners have taken an interest in industrial districts and clusters and their role in city growth and development by emphasizing the nature of the relationships among firms in a region as a source of clustering and juxtaposing local and global interactions in determining the role of cities in development	
Michael Porter and business strategy	Theory draws on neoclassical and social and institutional traditions as well as from business strategy. Describes industry clusters as the product of four factors (factor conditions, demand conditions, related and supporting industries, and firm strategy and competitiveness) termed "the diamond of competitive advantage." The diamond explains why clusters are more competitive than individual firms	Porter (1990, 2001, 2008)
Economic development practitioners	Examines the operation, development, and promotion of clusters producing practical insights into the nature of industrial agglomeration	Rosenfeld (1997)

Source: Cortright 2006.
a. This approach emphasizes the effects of social forces and relationships (such as customs, technological change, organizations, and social networks) that cannot be fully reduced to market decisions of individuals.

Figure 5.1 An Agribusiness Cluster

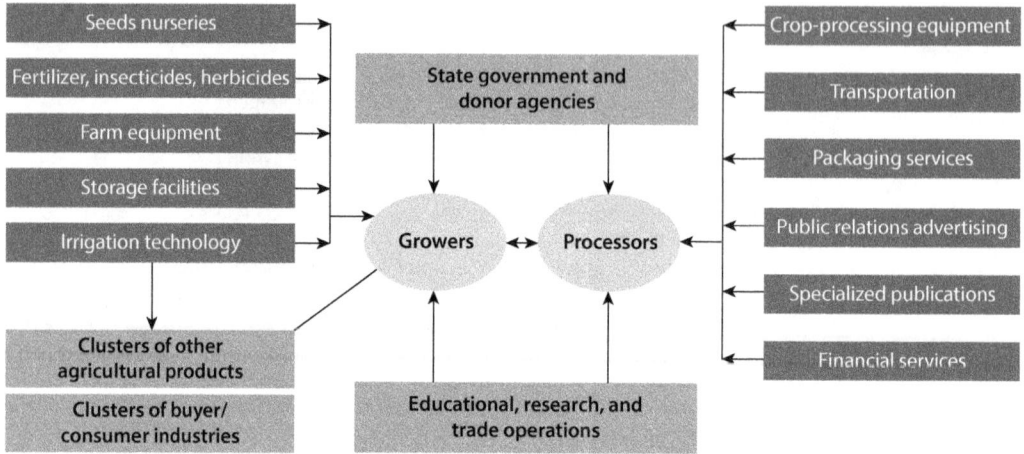

Source: World Bank 2009.

An industrial cluster represents an agglomeration of diverse actors—firms, suppliers, service providers, and related companies—in a specific industry. Figure 5.1 shows a typical cluster in the agribusiness sector.

In addition to the entities directly involved in the agribusiness sector, there are more tangential entities such as educational, research, and trade operations and state government and donor agencies. Geographic proximity as well as synergy from the activities of the various actors generates positive economic benefits such as "access to specialized human resources and suppliers, knowledge spill-overs, [and] pressure for higher performance in head-to-head competition" (World Bank 2009, 2).

Industrial clusters were used as a vehicle for productivity and as a means of enhancing the competitiveness of an area, a region, or a nation. The cluster concept is not new, but it is Porter's version that has gained widespread currency among policy makers, academics, and industrial organizations.[2]

Porter's definition of competitiveness grows out of an understanding of productivity as something that arises from "successful innovation in processes, or products, or both."[3] His discussion of clusters and competitiveness (Porter 2008, 9) emphasizes the following:

- Clusters increase productivity and efficiency.
- Clusters stimulate and enable innovations.
- Clusters facilitate commercialization and new business formation.

Clusters increase productivity and efficiency by facilitating efficient access to specialized inputs, services, employees, information, institutions, training programs, and other public goods. The existence of clusters increases the likelihood that opportunities for business will be recognized and also provides an environment in which businesses can come together to share knowledge and/ or create knowledge. Clusters help in bringing ideas to market (commercialization) because the opportunity for new products or processes is more apparent in clusters. Spin-off companies and start-ups are encouraged by the presence of other companies and the availability of skills and suppliers, for example.

Porter (2008, 6) defines the cluster as "a geographically proximate group of interconnected companies and associated institutions in a particular field, linked by commonalities and complementarities (external economies)." A cluster may contain

- an end-product industry or industries;
- downstream or channel industries;
- specialized suppliers;
- providers of specialized services;
- related industries (those with important shared activities, labor technologies, channels, or common customers);
- supporting institutions, including financial, training, standard setting, and research institutions as well as trade associations.

Examples of clusters in the United States are shown in table 5.3. The clusters listed are the three highest-ranking clusters in terms of share of national employment. The data are from the cluster mapping project at Harvard Business School.

Table 5.3 Regional Specialization—Clusters in the United States, 2008, Selected Geographic Areas

Geographic area	Cluster(s)		
Atlanta	Construction materials	Transportation and Logistics	Business services
Boston	Analytical instruments	Education and knowledge creation	Communications equipment
Chicago	Communications equipment	Processed food	Heavy machinery
Denver	Leather and sporting goods	Oil and gas	Aerospace vehicles and defense
Houston	Oil and gas production and services	Chemical products	Heavy construction services
Los Angeles	Apparel	Building fixtures, equipment, and Services	Entertainment
Pittsburgh	Construction materials	Metal manufacturing	Education and knowledge creation
Raleigh-Durham	Communications equipment	Information technology	Education and knowledge creation
San Diego	Leather and sporting goods	Power generation	Education and knowledge creation
San Francisco-Oakland-San Jose Bay Area	Communications equipment	Agricultural products	Information technology
Seattle-Bellevue-Everett	Aerospace vehicles and defense	Fishing and fishing products	Analytical instruments
Wichita	Aerospace vehicles and defense	Heavy machinery	Oil and gas

Source: Porter 2008.

Clusters of Competitiveness • http://dx.doi.org/10.1596/978-1-4648-0049-8

Figure 5.2 Determinants of Innovative Capacity

Innovative capactiy

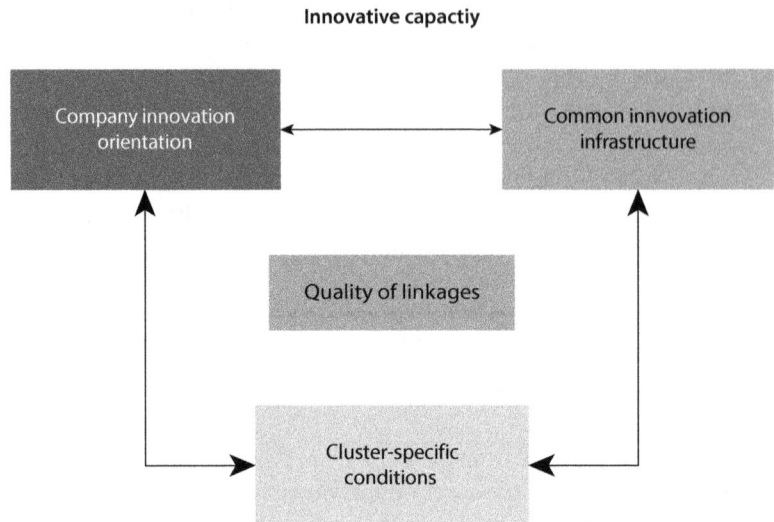

The success of industrial clusters depends among other things on their capacity to innovate, whether it be the technological innovation that characterizes the information technology (IT) clusters in Silicon Valley and Bangalore or the creative innovation representative of the fashion design clusters in Paris and Mumbai (World Bank 2009). The determinants of innovative capacity are outlined in figure 5.2. The innovative capacity of the company depends very much upon the quality of the links between the innovative orientation and potential of the company and the cluster-specific conditions.

Productivity growth for Porter arises from the interactions between the four factors in his diamond model: firm strategy, structure, and rivalry; input factor conditions; demand conditions; and the presence of related and supporting industries. The diamond is shown in figure 5.3.

The interface between firms in a geographic area is primarily one of competitive rivalry although collaboration can also be important.[4] Geographical proximity affects competitiveness in three ways:

1. It increases productivity—firms can operate with lower levels of stock because of the local presence of specialized suppliers, and they have access to specialized skills and human resources, aided by specialized and local training providers.
2. It increases the capacity for innovation by facilitating interaction and the dissemination of knowledge—competition between firms raises the incentive to innovate, which in turn raises the capacity to adapt to changes and external shocks.
3. It stimulates and enables new business formation through spin-off enterprises that face lower barriers to entry than in other localities—this in turn creates

Figure 5.3 Productivity and the Business Environment

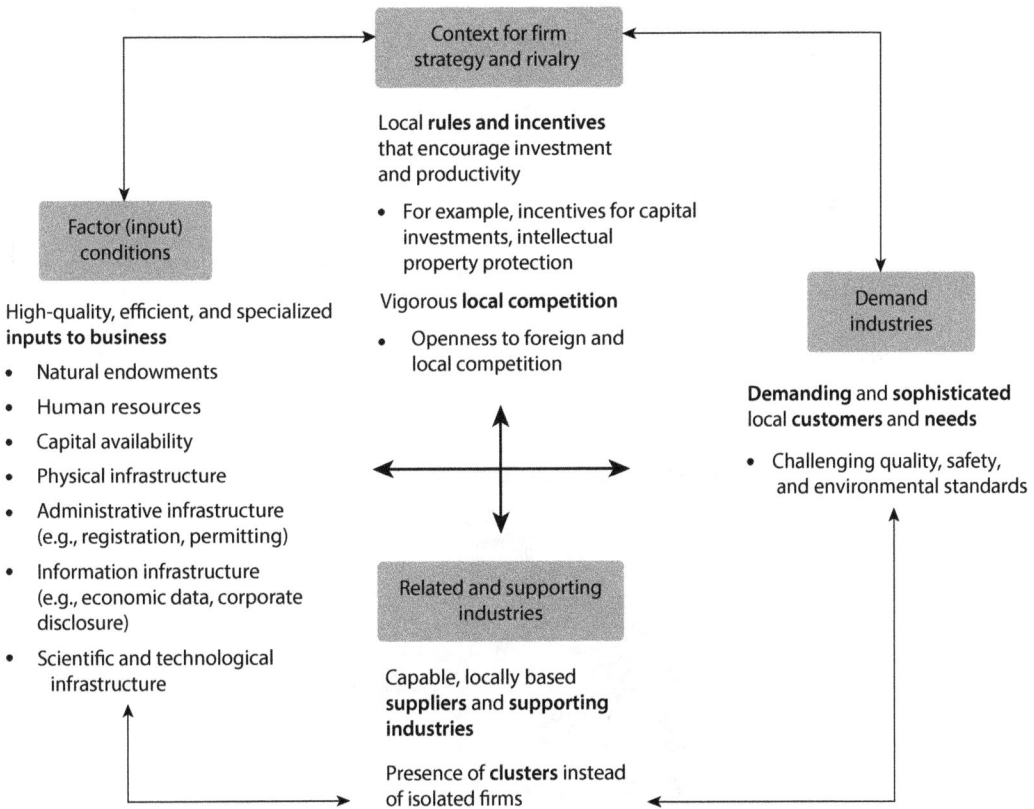

Context for firm
strategy and rivalry

Local **rules and incentives**
that encourage investment
and productivity

- For example, incentives for capital
  investments, intellectual
  property protection

Factor (input)
conditions

Vigorous **local competition**

- Openness to foreign and
  local competition

Demand
industries

High-quality, efficient, and specialized
inputs to business

- Natural endowments
- Human resources
- Capital availability
- Physical infrastructure
- Administrative infrastructure
  (e.g., registration, permitting)
- Information infrastructure
  (e.g., economic data, corporate
  disclosure)
- Scientific and technological
  infrastructure

Demanding and **sophisticated**
local **customers** and **needs**

- Challenging quality, safety,
  and environmental standards

Related and supporting
industries

Capable, locally based
suppliers and **supporting
industries**

Presence of **clusters** instead
of isolated firms

Source: Porter et al. 2008. © World Economic Forum. Used with permission; further permission required for reuse.

a positive feedback loop through more competition, innovation, and so on
(see note 3).

Industrial clusters are not confined to one particular geographic area but may
instead span regional or national boundaries. In fact, Porter (2008) noted that a
region's clusters were also likely to be present in neighboring regions. Export-
oriented clusters tend to have a lower share of employment but higher average
wages, productivity, and innovation (table 5.4). Traded clusters—those clusters
made up of traded industries—account for just over 29 percent of employment,
compared to 70 percent for local clusters. However, the average wage in the
traded clusters was almost $50,000, compared to just over $30,000 in the local
clusters.

Globalization has been positive for cluster development. As markets globalize,
firms have a choice of where to locate. As resources flow to given areas, the role
of clusters is reinforced and regional specialization ensues. Ketels, Lindqvist, and
Sölvell (2008) suggest that this process leads to clusters becoming increasingly
specialized and increasingly connected with other clusters. Moreover, clusters that
are successful are more likely to participate in the global marketplace and connect

Table 5.4 Composition of Regional Economies, United States, 2004

	Traded clusters	Local clusters	Natural resource–driven industries
Number	40	19	n.a.
Share of employment (%)	29.3	70.0	0.7
Employment growth 1990–2004 (%)	0.7	2.4	−1.2
Average wage	$49,367	$30,416	$35,815
Relative wage (%)	137.2	84.5	99.5
Wage growth (%)	4.2	3.4	2.1
Relative productivity	144.1	79.3	140.1
Patents per 10,000 employees	23.0	0.4	3.3
Number of SIC	590	241	48

Source: Porter 2008.
Note: n.a. = not applicable; SIC = standard industrial classification.

Figure 5.4 Dimensions of Clusters and Economic Policy

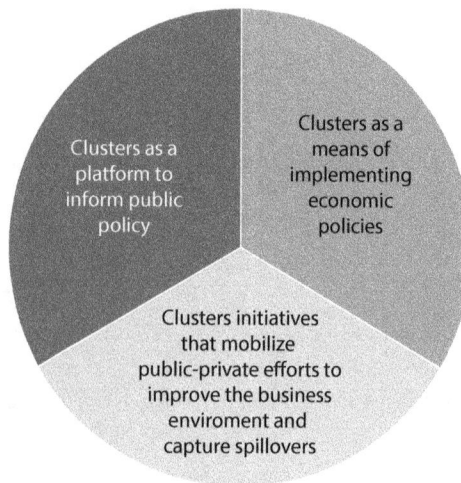

Source: Porter 2008. © Michael E. Porter. Used with permission; further permission required for reuse.

with other clusters providing complementary activities. As shown in figure 5.3, the existence of one cluster may beget another. World Bank (2009, 3) identifies the optics cluster in Arizona as one that subsequently gave rise to clusters in "plastics, aerospace, environment technologies, information technologies and biosciences."

The role of government is important, particularly in regard to the regulatory environment for business and national policies that affect education and skills. Porter (2008) suggests that the old model of economic development, predicated on government driving economic development through policy decisions and incentives, is redundant. The new model understands economic development as a collaborative process involving government at multiple levels, as well as companies, teaching and research institutions, and institutions for collaboration. Clusters have a significant role to play in this new model, as shown in figure 5.4.

Cluster Initiatives

"Cluster initiatives are organized efforts to increase the growth and competitiveness of clusters within a region, involving cluster firms, government and/or the research community" (Sölvell, Lindqvist, and Ketels 2003). Findings from the Global Cluster Initiative Survey (Sölvell, Lindqvist, and Ketels 2003) suggest that "almost all Cluster Initiatives have a dedicated facilitator and many (68%) have some sort of office. Many (78%) spend time and efforts to build a framework of shared ideas about why the Cluster Initiative is beneficial and how it is supposed to work" (Ketels, Lindqvist, and Sölvell 2008, 7).[5] Intelligence on how things are supposed to work comes from an examination of the clusters' own strengths and capabilities. Most CIs formulate a plan. Dialogue between the various stakeholders is key to forming new partnerships between cluster leaders and the various public sector organizations.

The different CIs have different objectives, but each engages in formally organized efforts with the government and the private sector. Examples of objectives include the following:

- Facilitating market development through joint market assessment, marketing, and brand building;
- Encouraging relationship building (networking) within the cluster, within the region, and with clusters in other locations;
- Promoting collaborative innovation—research, product and process development, and commercialization;
- Aiding the innovation diffusion, that is, the adoption of innovative products, processes, and practices;
- Supporting the cluster's expansion through attracting firms to the area and supporting new business development;
- Sponsoring education and training activities;
- Representing cluster interests before external organizations such as regional development partnerships; national trade associations; and local, state, and federal governments (Mills, Reynolds, and Reamer 2008).

The range of objectives is quite broad, and CIs tend to cover four to five main objectives. Older CIs tend to be more narrowly focused compared to younger CIs (Ketels, Lindqvist, and Sölvell 2008).

World Bank (2009) provides an overview of one approach to developing a CI. As figure 5.5 shows, the first stage of development involves mapping and engagement with stakeholders; in the second stage, 10 cluster tools are applied to identify gaps in the cluster's competitive position and to aid in developing collaboration and collective business strategies among the cluster members.[6] In the third stage, leader cluster members then form partnerships with various public sector organizations to expedite policy reform in areas such as industrial development, infrastructure development, research, innovation, and training. Finally, in the fourth stage, the industrial links formed through clusters provide a solid basis

Figure 5.5 One Approach to Developing a Cluster Initiative

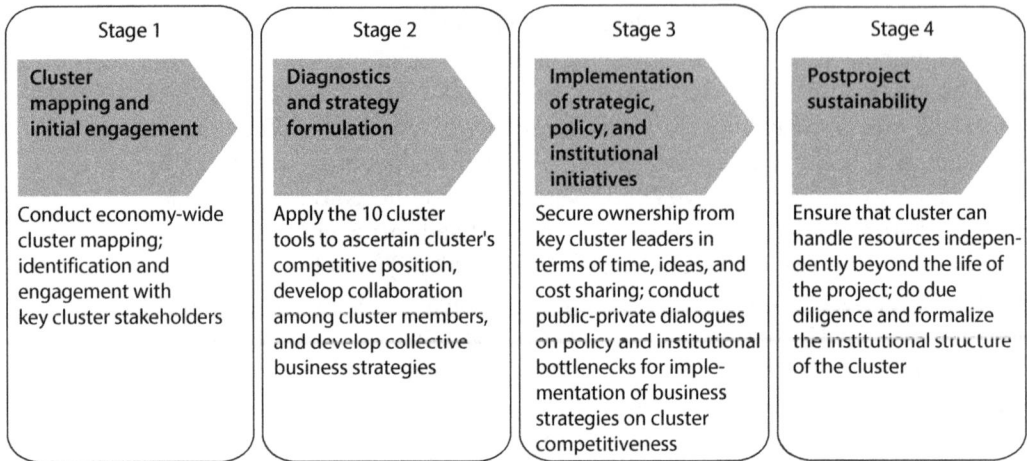

Stage 1	Stage 2	Stage 3	Stage 4
Cluster mapping and initial engagement	Diagnostics and strategy formulation	Implementation of strategic, policy, and institutional initiatives	Postproject sustainability
Conduct economy-wide cluster mapping; identification and engagement with key cluster stakeholders	Apply the 10 cluster tools to ascertain cluster's competitive position, develop collaboration among cluster members, and develop collective business strategies	Secure ownership from key cluster leaders in terms of time, ideas, and cost sharing; conduct public-private dialogues on policy and institutional bottlenecks for implementation of business strategies on cluster competitiveness	Ensure that cluster can handle resources independently beyond the life of the project; do due diligence and formalize the institutional structure of the cluster

Source: World Bank 2009.

for the formulation and sequencing of policy reforms. CIs become in effect a tool for government in pursuing policy reform because "together they [CIs and policy reform] may create positive externalities by informing government of the policy implications and possible business responses" (World Bank 2009, 5).

The GCIS (2003) suggested that CIs are initiated by government in 32 percent of cases, by industry in 27 percent, or equally by both in 35 percent. Slightly over half of financing comes primarily from government (54 percent of cases), while companies are the most influential parties in the governance of CIs (Ketels, Lindqvist, and Sölvell 2008). While clusters may evolve naturally, a CI can hasten the process and concentrate on the areas in which policy and institutional impediments may be hindering competitiveness. Some key areas of focus include "market information, workforce development, supply chain improvements, quality standards, branding, forward integration, and process improvements" (World Bank 2009, 4).

The number of CIs has increased significantly over time. The 2003 GCIS identified over 500 CIs across Europe, North America, Australia, and New Zealand, and the number has likely grown since then.[7] *The Cluster Initiative Greenbook* (Sölvell, Lindqvist, and Ketels, 2003) reports the following:

- The performance of CIs is measured along three dimensions—innovation and international competitiveness; cluster growth; and goal fulfillment. In all, 85 percent agree that the CI has improved the competitiveness of the cluster it was set up to serve, and 89 percent report that the CI helped the cluster grow. About 81 percent of CIs have met their goals.
- The national social, political, and economic setting within which each CI is implemented is important for the performance.[8]
- CIs serving strong clusters of national and regional importance are more successful than those serving weaker clusters.

- CIs initiated through a competition process to get government financing perform significantly better in terms of increasing international competitiveness.[9]
- CIs limited to domestic companies perform worse than those that are not limited.
- CIs with offices and budgets sufficient to conduct significant projects without seeking separate funding perform better than those that lack them.[10]
- For the facilitator, having a broad network of contacts is the most important success factor, but the facilitator's qualities are more important for competitiveness performance than for growth performance.
- CIs that build a clear, explicit framework, based on the cluster's own strengths, and that spend time to share this framework with all parties, are clearly more successful in promoting cluster competitiveness than those that do not take these steps.
- Generally, disappointing results for CIs, including the failure to generate changes, are related to poor consensus, weak frameworks, facilitators lacking strong networks, lack of offices and sufficient budgets, and neglected brand building. Disappointing CIs tend to involve less important clusters.
- Government policy and other setting factors also influence performance indirectly, by affecting the objectives CIs pursue and some process issues. For example, in countries where local government decision makers are important, CIs tend to pay more attention to various competitiveness-related objectives, such as promoting new technology and monitoring technical trends.

The setting of each CI depends upon the *country's* underlying level of economic development, which has implications for the range of objectives and the manner in which each CI is initiated, financed, and organized. CIs are therefore country- and industry-specific but are most common in developed and transition economies. They tend to focus on technology-intensive areas "like IT, medical devices, production technology, communications equipment, biopharmaceuticals, and automotive" (Ketels, Lindqvist, and Sölvell 2008,6).

CIs and cluster-based competitiveness projects have been associated with advanced economies since the mid-1990s, and have been part of the economic development framework for developing and transition economies since the year 2000. International donor organizations have become involved in and have initiated CIs. In fact, donor-initiated CIs are located in the most challenging settings, even in relation to CIs in developing and transition economies. Donor-initiated CIs, which operate in locations where there is little national policy support for CIs, help circumvent some of the trust issues prevalent in developing and transition economies.[11] Because policy is more likely to be centralized in developing and transition economies and preoccupied with macroeconomic issues, "there is usually little policy support relating to competitiveness and clusters" (Ketels, Lindqvist, and Sölvell, 2006, 5).

"Cluster Initiatives in developing countries face very different challenges and often have different types of specific objectives compared to those in transition

Table 5.5 Comparison of Cluster Initiatives by Level of Economic Development

Measure	Type of economy		
	Developing	Transition	Advanced
Objectives	CIs focus on supply chain development, export promotion Increasing value-added, improving business environment	Donor-initiated CIs have a narrower range—export promotion and increasing value-added	CIs focus on innovation and business environment improvement
Activities	Upgrading human resources, developing supply chain, and working out joint logistics	Lobbying for changes in business environment; management training; supply chain development	Firm formation; high importance of joint R&D
Membership and resources	71% of CIs have an office; 37% have a website; median of 3 staff members	Fewer companies participating in CIs—median number is 18 with just 40% of CIs having more than 20 companies 62% of CIs have an office; 41% have a website; median of 2 staff members	CIs are larger, 51% have more than 20 firms participating and median is 25 companies 75% of CIs have an office; 79% have a website; median of 2 staff members
Cluster focus	Focus on "basic" industries	More of a mix of industry types; but donor initiators focus on "basic" industries and agriculture	Sometimes a tendency to favor "high-tech" industries
Role of government and financing	CIs often have an international initiator; government initiatives are also frequent; those initiated by business are less frequent International funding is usually the main source of income for CIs	Largest share of funding comes from business sector	Dominating role of government that leaves business on the sidelines of CIs is a concern Most of financing for CIs is provided by government
Performance	Developing economies score best in acquiring funds and improving the business environment, followed by export promotion	CIs in transition economies report their best results in acquiring funds from government and international organizations, improving business environment and increasing innovativeness	CIs in advanced economies score best in increasing innovativeness

Source: Compiled from Ketels, Lindqvist, and Sölvell 2006.
Note: CI = cluster initiative; R&D = research and development.

economies, and there is no simple linear relationship from developing to transition to advanced economies"[12] (Ketels, Lindqvist, and Sölvell 2006, 5). Table 5.5 compares CIs in advanced, developing, and transition economies on a range of measures. The information is compiled "from a survey of 1,400 cluster initiatives, including comprehensive data from 450 CIs that completed the Global Cluster Initiative Survey [in] 2005," as reported in Ketels, Lindqvist, and Sölvell (2006, 5).

The main findings from the global survey may be summarized by the following:

Each CI must find the approach that will be most effective by taking into consideration the level of development of the economy (developing, transition, or advanced) and the barriers to competitiveness faced by each cluster. Removing barriers to competitiveness depends upon the country's economic policy agenda. The environment for CIs is more accepting, if clusters are accepted as a tool for economic development and if competitiveness is part of an economic development plan—locally, regionally, or nationally.

Greater centralization of decision making in transition and developing economies has implications for cluster development and CIs. First, clusters are essentially a local phenomenon that benefit from the involvement of local and regional government. CIs will be compromised by insufficient decision-making power at the local level (see bars "a" in figure 5.6). Second, "competitiveness and clusters play less of a role in economic policy" in transition economies than in others (bars "b" and "c" in figure 5.6; Ketels, Lindqvist, and Sölvell 2006, 29). This may be due to a greater emphasis on macroeconomic policy in these countries. On the other hand, developing, transition, and advanced countries all consider competitiveness an important issue in the economic policy debate (bars "d" in figure 5.6).

CIs in transition and developing economies operate in a more challenging environment than those in advanced economies because of the low levels of trust and an economic policy that is less oriented toward competitiveness and clusters. The overall success of the cluster depends upon trust between the various participants in the cluster. Trust improves as economic development progresses, although trust between firms and government in transition economies is lower than in developing economies (figure 5.7). CIs are stymied in low-trust environments, both in

Figure 5.6 Policy Setting in which CIs Are Conducted

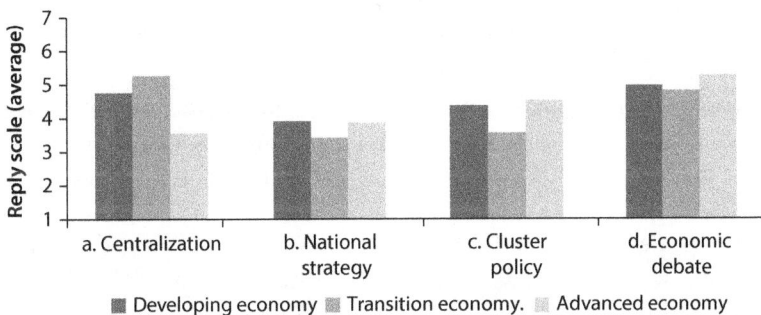

■ Developing economy ■ Transition economy. ■ Advanced economy

Source: Ketels, Lindqvist, and Sölvell 2006, 29. © Christian Ketels, Göran Lindqvist, and Örjan Sölvell. Used with permission; further permission required for reuse.
Note: CI = cluster initiative. The sets of bars show responses to survey questions by cluster initiative facilitators, indicating agreement on a scale of 1 (disagree completely) to 7 (agree completely). (a) Economic development policy is driven by initiatives at the national government level, not at the local/regional level. (b) The national government has a clear strategy for improving competitiveness. (c) Cluster policies are a core element in economic development policy. (d) Competitiveness is a key issue in the economic policy debate.

Figure 5.7 Level of Trust between Firms and between the Private and Public Sector

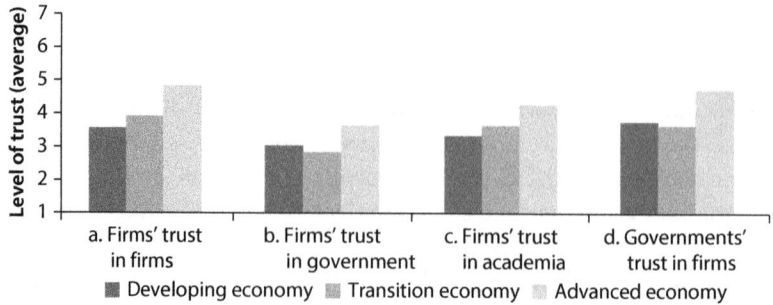

Source: Ketels, Lindqvist, and Sölvell 2006. © Christian Ketels, Göran Lindqvist, and Örjan Sölvell. Used with permission; further permission required for reuse.
Note: The sets of bars show responses to survey questions, indicating agreement on a scale of 1 (disagree completely) to 7 (agree completely). (a) Firms' trust in other firms; (b) firms' trust in government initiative; (c) firms' trust in academia; and (d) Government trusts in firms.

Figure 5.8 Objectives Considered Most Important for the CI

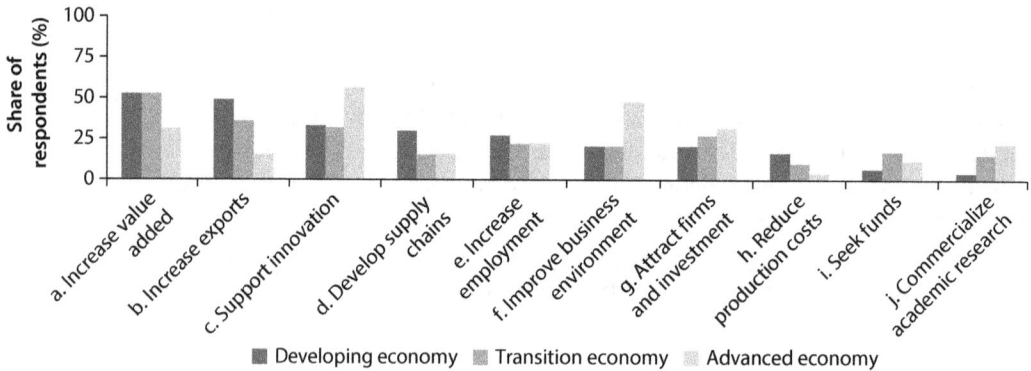

Source: Ketels, Lindqvist, and Sölvell 2006. © Christian Ketels, Göran Lindqvist, and Örjan Sölvell. Used with permission; further permission required for reuse.
Note: CI = cluster initiative. The sets of bars show the percentage of survey respondents who ranked the objective as one of the three most important.

how effectively they can operate and in beginning to operate in the first place. Among advanced economies, where trust is highest, CIs can develop an action plan from the beginning. CIs also represent an important vehicle for increasing trust over time.

CIs in developing and transition countries usually have different objectives from those in advanced economies. The survey found that CIs in developing and transition economies emphasize value added and exports, whereas CIs in advanced economies emphasize innovation and improving the business environment. Figure 5.8 shows which objectives are considered among the most important by respondents categorized by economy type. Ketels, Lindqvist, and Sölvell (2006) suggest that the differences in objectives may be related to the lack of local government involvement in developing and transition economies.

Firms in these economies focus on aspects of competitiveness that they can affect, such as in-house activities.

Selecting the right cluster for each CI will depend among other things on the type of industry and the strength of cluster. The type of industry is given when the CI is initiated by the business sector itself. The industry needs to be selected for CIs when the government or donor is the initiator. For developing countries in particular, and for transition economies, "basic" industries—agriculture, food, and basic manufacturing—are the most common type of industry in CIs and particularly where donors are the initiators. Figure 5.9 shows the target industries. High-tech industries are more dominant in advanced country CIs. Transition country CIs are spread across the various industrial sectors. The pattern shown in figure 5.9 may reflect the general industry profile in the underlying economies; that is, we would expect there to be a lot of basic industries in developing economies and a lot of high-tech industries in the advanced economies. Whether this pattern reflects a bias on behalf of the CIs is a separate research question and a valid one.

What is understood by the concept of a "strong" cluster differs depending on the economic development of the underlying country. CIs target strong clusters, and in advanced economies this usually means clusters with a strong competitive position and capacity to innovate (see figure 5.10). Donors in transition countries tend to target those clusters that are less developed than those targeted by government and/or the business sector. Figure 5.10 shows the various dimensions that can measure the strength of a cluster.

CIs target clusters that have global market reach, economic importance, and growth potential, with little difference across the remaining dimensions, except, as noted above, the competitive position and the capacity for innovation. Differences do arise when comparing the clusters targeted by donors to those targeted by government and/or the business sector in developing and transition counties (figure 5.11).

Figure 5.9 Target Industries Selected by Donors or Government for the Purposes of CIs

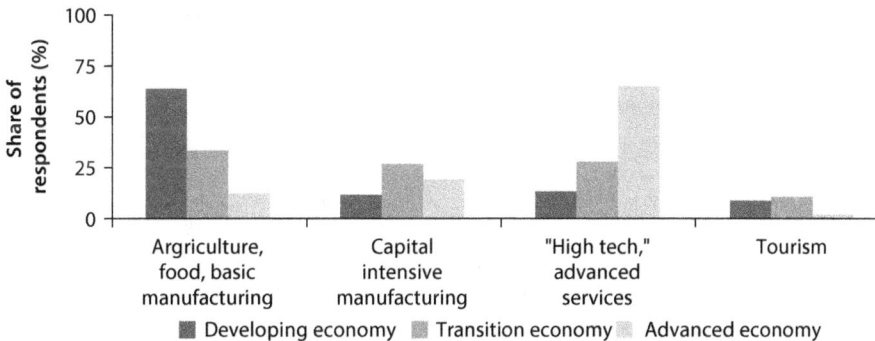

Source: Ketels, Lindqvist, and Sölvell 2006. © Christian Ketels, Göran Lindqvist, and Örjan Sölvell. Used with permission; further permission required for reuse.
Note: CI = cluster initiative. The sets of bars show the percentage of survey respondents (government or donors) targeting industries (for the purposes of cluster initiatives) in developing, transition, and advanced economies.

Figure 5.10 Cluster Strength

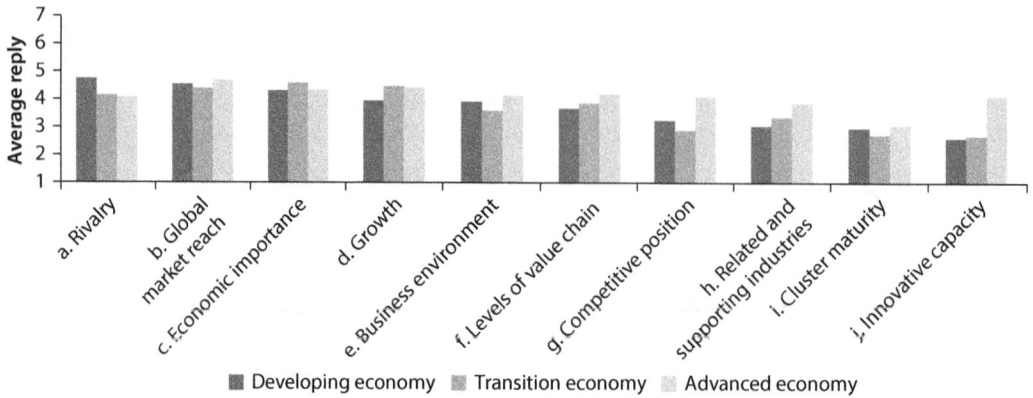

Source: Ketels, Lindqvist, and Sölvell 2006, 33. © Christian Ketels, Göran Lindqvist, and Örjan Sölvell. Used with permission; further permission required for reuse.
Note: Facilitators from the cluster initiatives (CIs) were asked about the strength of their clusters measured along many different dimensions. The sets of bars show responses to survey questions, indicating ratings on a scale of 1 (weak) to 7 (strong). (a) How strong is the cluster based on rivalry (i.e., who are the major players in your industry?)? (b) How strong is the cluster based on global market reach (sales to global markets)? (c) How strong is the cluster based on its economic importance (to the nation)? (d) How strong is the cluster based on its growth performance? (e) How strong is the cluster based on the business environment? (f) How strong is the cluster based on levels of the value chain? (g) How strong is the cluster based on its competitive position? (h) How strong is the cluster based on the range of related and supporting industries? (i) How strong is the cluster based on its level of maturity? (j) How strong is the cluster based on its innovative capacity?"

Figure 5.11 Cluster Strength by Initiator—Developing and Transition Countries

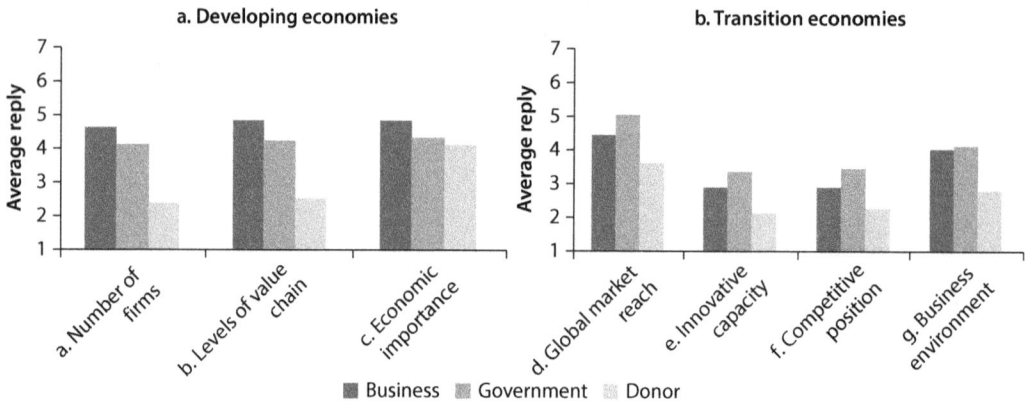

Source: Ketels, Lindqvist, and Sölvell 2006. © Christian Ketels, Göran Lindqvist, and Örjan Sölvell. Used with permission; further permission required for reuse.
Note: Cluster facilitators were asked about the strength of their clusters measured along many different dimensions. Results were compiled into three categories based on whether the cluster initiatives (CIs) came from the business community, the government, or the donor. The sets of bars show the responses from business, government, and donor CIs from developing countries (figure on left-hand side) and transition economies (figure on right-hand side) to survey questions, indicating ratings on a scale of 1 (weak) to 7 (strong). (a) How strong is the cluster based on the number of firms? (b) How strong is the cluster based on the number of levels of value chain? (c) How strong is the cluster based on its economic importance (to the nation)? (d) How strong is the cluster based on its global market reach? (e) How strong is the cluster based on its innovative capacity? (f) How strong is the cluster based on its competitive position? (g) How strong is the cluster based on the business environment?

Donors in developing countries target clusters that have fewer firms and fewer levels of the value chain and that are less economically important to the nation as a whole. In transition countries, donors target clusters that have less global market reach, less innovative capacity, weaker competitive position, and a less favorable business environment. The reasons for these findings are unclear; they may relate to the environment in which the donor operates, for example.

The principle aim of CIs is to address barriers to competition. These barriers may arise from shortcomings in the business, government, or education sectors (Ketels, Lindqvist, and Sölvell 2006). These sectors are represented in CIs in various degrees. For example, government often plays a dominant role in advanced economies; see figure 5.12. This is less true of developing and transition economies, where the business sector and donors take the lead. Part of the reason may well be that the capacity of government to launch CIs is weak in these economies, so that donors step in to fill this void.

Ketels, Lindqvist, and Sölvell (2006) further examine what occurs after the initiation of clusters—does government step back and allow the business sector to take over or does it remain heavily involved? The scenario for all three types of economy—developing, transition, and advanced—is similar: "Government influence decreases over time while business becomes more important" (Ketels, Lindqvist, and Sölvell 2006, 36). Figure 5.13 shows which sector—government, business, or donor—was the most influential in determining which initial activities to undertake. Among advanced economies, government was the primary initiator and remained dominant in selecting the initial participants in the CI; but it then transferred out when the time came to decide initial activities. This was deemed a good pattern by Ketels, Lindqvist, and Sölvell (2006). The decreasing role of government was also seen in developing and transition economies. The situation with donors was a little different; donors remained

Figure 5.12 Entity Responsible for Initiating CI by Economy's Underlying Level of Development

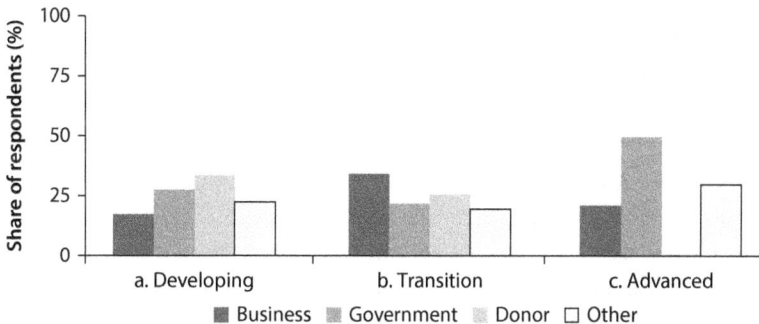

Source: Ketels, Lindqvist, and Sölvell 2006. © Christian Ketels, Göran Lindqvist, and Örjan Sölvell. Used with permission; further permission required for reuse.
Note: The sets of bars show the percentage of cluster initiatives (CIs) by initiator (business, government, donor, or other) classified by type of economy: (a) developing, (b) transition, and (c) advanced.

Figure 5.13 Influence in First Stage of Cluster Initiatives' Operation, by Sector and Economy Type

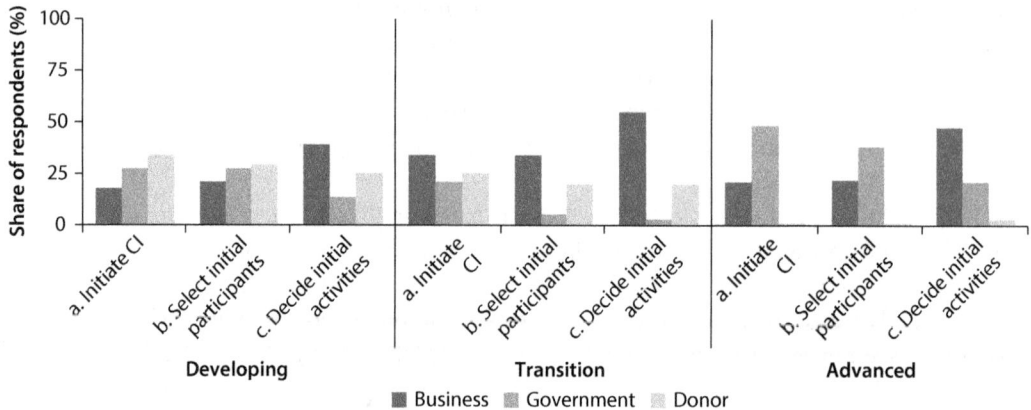

Source: Ketels, Lindqvist, and Sölvell 2006, 36. © Christian Ketels, Göran Lindqvist, and Örjan Sölvell. Used with permission; further permission required for reuse.

Note: Percentages do not sum to 100 because data for "other actors" are not shown. The sets of bars show the percentage of cluster initiatives (CIs) by initiator (business, government, donor, or other) classified by the initiator's decisions in the early stages to (a) initiate the CI, (b) select initial participants, and (c) decide initial activities and by each type of economy; developing, transition, and. advanced.

heavily involved in the initial stage of CIs, though "in the longer run, . . . donor-initiated CIs appear to allow as much business sector influence as government, or even more" (Ketels, Lindqvist, and Sölvell 2006, 36). The challenge for donors in the short run is to also address the weaknesses in local and regional government institutions for which they are compensating by becoming involved in CIs. Donors fulfill the role of government in transition and developing economies—but there are limits to their involvement; they fail to address the underlying weaknesses in the business environment, and they are often influenced by their need to provide measurable results in a short time, often as short as 3 years. CIs should be used when long-term competitiveness is the goal and not short-term results such as increased employment or exports (Ketels, Lindqvist, and Sölvell 2006, 5).

Policy Implications

World Bank (2009) outlines how the existence of clusters helps to guide policy makers in forming policies for competitiveness. For example, government involvement in clusters can help identify barriers to competition and put in place policies to address these. Specialized inputs and skills are easier to access and are cheaper when firms are organized in a cluster setting, and public information and knowledge are more readily disseminated. Quasi-public goods such as infrastructure, educational programs, and trade fairs are easier for government to oversee at the cluster level compared to the macro or regional level. Finally, clusters perform a useful search function in identifying those firms and industries that are not performing as well as others, thus providing valuable information for government and the business sector.

The many factors affecting competitiveness arise from the macroeconomy in general and the microeconomic environment of the firm specifically. Forces affecting these factors are constantly changing, rendering competitiveness a dynamic concept. As such, policy for competitiveness is multifaceted. Macroeconomic policy alone, while necessary, is not sufficient for improving competitiveness. Macro policy needs to be aware of its effect on how firms and markets operate. Furthermore, globalization has changed the way in which firms and markets operate, with greater technological absorption by firms and global integration by markets (World Bank 2009). On the microeconomic side, competitiveness is no longer primarily associated with price and cost but includes "connectivity, standards and certifications, quality and innovation, exploitation of cultural and geographic endowments, success of branding, etc." (World Bank 2009, 67). Policy for competitiveness needs to be mindful of these changes and engage agents/institutions at many levels and from both public and private sector backgrounds. Being able to move forward with competitiveness policies to improve competitiveness requires a solid regime "to ensure that resources flow to the industrial clusters that have the best comparative advantage, and within those, to the firms that are economically most efficient" (World Bank 2009, 68).

Each country will have its own issues that impact negatively on the competitiveness of its firms and economy. The World Economic Forum's *Global Competitiveness Report* (Porter et al. 2008) outlines the barriers to competitiveness at the country level. The stage of development has implications for the 12 pillars of competitiveness outlined in the report. The Global Competitiveness Index highlights three stages of development—factor-driven economies, efficiency-driven economies, and innovation-driven economies. At the high-income level, companies must compete by producing new and innovative products. At the middle-income level, firms tend to concentrate on fairly sophisticated interventions and the formation of firm-level and supply chain strategies. At the lower-income country level, efforts may concentrate on improving market and government imperfections in factor markets and demand conditions. Despite this, there is no road map, and the respective roles of the private and public sector in formulating policy for competitiveness are unclear. Imperfect information characterizes both the government and the business sector.

The formation of CIs provides a valuable resource for policy makers in helping to identify the barriers to competitiveness. The involvement of both public and private sector actors renders the CI a fertile place in which to identify policy issues, which can then be brought to the attention of policy makers. Porter's diamond analysis provides a framework for identifying policy reforms, while technical tools such as "value-chain analysis, market-trend analysis, and competitiveness positioning analyses can ascertain operational efficiency of such reforms" (World Bank 2009, 77). Finally, the CI provides a forum for the development of a detailed policy map with suggestions on the most effective way to implement reforms. Table 5.6 shows the possible policy and strategic recommendations that may emanate from a CI.

Table 5.6 Possible Policy and Strategic Recommendations from a Cluster Initiative

	Public policy recommendations	Private sector business strategy recommendations
Cluster-specific	• Remove entry/exit barriers in industries related to the cluster • Remove regulatory burdens that prevent firms from functioning efficiently • Develop institutions that cater to the collective R&D needs of firms in the cluster • Develop institutions that offer specialized skills for competitiveness • One-stop shop for dissemination of public information on products and markets • Facilitate export promotion and FDI attraction • Develop provisions for basic provisions such as land, labor, and capital as well as advanced factors such as skilled labor, technology and equipment, faster/ cheaper transportation, etc.	• Identify new product and market segments and develop business strategies for increased outreach • Shop floor enhancements of technology and management for higher productivity • Improve the capacity of specialized input and service providers • Market research • Promotion of specific products in the local, regional, and international markets • Develop semiprivate institutions such as business associations, research and advisory centers, knowledge transfer centers, etc.
Economy-wide	• Restructure the incentive regime and set up performance measurement systems as necessary • Develop basic infrastructure necessary for industries to function • Develop sound institutions that contribute to the capitalization of natural and socioeconomic endowments • Develop strong human capital • Expedite overall regulatory reform	• Increase private sector investments in infrastructure and services • Strengthen private sector capacity to smooth and sophisticate the overall supply chain • Develop strong, competitive institutions for training and R&D

Source: World Bank 2009.
Note: FDI = Foreign Direct Investment; R&D = research and development.

Conclusion

The chapter discussed clusters and competitiveness by focusing initially on the definition of and background to the cluster concept, highlighting its application to competitiveness, and then examining the role for government in promoting and developing CIs. The chapter concluded with a discussion of the policy implications of clusters for competitiveness.

Clusters are a means of stimulating economic development at the local, regional, and global level. They play an important role in the modern economy and its search for competitiveness. Clusters arise at many different levels and for many different areas of economic activity. The chapter focused on industrial clusters and looked at the advantages of these for competitiveness; it also presented examples of clusters. It looked at the implications of industrial clusters for both the sector and the geographical area. The former analysis focused on the links between firm strategy, structure, and rivalry; input factor conditions; demand conditions; and the presence of related supportive industries. The cluster concept spans the local, regional, national, and international arena, and the chapter looked at these links across geographic space. A key factor in industrial clusters was innovation.

The second part of the chapter examined CIs, which are organized efforts to increase growth and competitiveness within a region and are also a tool for government in pursuing policy reform. Following an example of an approach to developing a CI, the chapter presented the characteristics of successful CIs. CIs were compared based on the level of economic development of the underlying economy. Differences were seen in objectives, target industries, cluster strength, the types of initiator (donor or government), and their influence. Finally, the chapter noted that the existence of clusters helps to guide policy makers in forming policies for competitiveness. The chapter concluded with a description of public policy and private sector implications of CIs.

Notes

1. See Nallari, Griffith, and Yusuf (2012) for a discussion of creative cities and knowledge cities.

2. Alfred Marshall (1920) suggested a threefold classification of the reasons for industrial concentration nearly a century ago. In Nallari, Griffith, and Yusuf's (2012, 8) paraphrase, he suggested that concentration arises because of "(a) knowledge spillovers, (b) the advantages of thick markets for specialized skills, and (c) the backward and forward linkages associated with large local markets."

   Note also that "what Porter called 'clusters' have been labeled by economic geographers variously as: 'industrial districts', 'new industrial spaces', 'regional industrial complexes', or, 'innovative milieux'—to name but a few. The exact terminology depends on particular theoretical perspectives or research interests." Local Government Association, "Industrial Clusters and Their Implications for Local Economic Policy." http://www.idea.gov.uk/idk/core/page.do?pageId=8507296#contents-1.

3. Local Government Association, "Industrial Clusters and Their Implications for Local Economic Policy." http://www.idea.gov.uk/idk/core/page.do?pageId=8507296#contents-1.

4. Firms of a similar type might support trade or professional associations that may help in disseminating best practice and lead to an upgrading of skills.

5. The Global Cluster Initiative Survey (GCIS) 2003 "identified more than 500 cluster initiatives around the world, primarily in Europe, North America, New Zealand and Australia. 238 completed the on-line survey, representing a broad range of technology areas" (Sölvell, Lindqvist, and Ketels 2003, 10). The survey covered the (1) setting, (2) objectives, (3) process, and (4) performance of the cluster initiatives.

6. The 10 tools are (1) cluster mapping; (2) product and market segmentation; (3) SWOT (strengths, weaknesses, opportunities, and threats); (4) Gap analysis (comparing actual performance with potential performance); (5) Porter's five forces analysis; (6) value chain analysis; (7) market trends analysis; (8) competitive positioning analysis; (9) old and new institutions for collaboration; and (10) monitoring and evaluation (World Bank 2009).

7. In 2008, Mills, Reynolds, and Reamer said that the number of cluster initiatives (CIs) had "expanded significantly in the last five years" and referred to the "several hundred distinct cluster initiatives" in the United States (14). They identified the following specific initiatives: Cleveland's WIRE-net; the St. Louis BioBelt; Florida's Technology Coast Manufacturing and Engineering Network; Southeast Michigan's Automation Alley; Oregon Metals Initiative; and the Massachusetts Life Sciences Collaborative.

8. "Key factors include a high level of company trust in government initiatives and having influential local government decision makers, which are both clearly related to good Cluster Initiative performance" (Ketels, Lindqvist, and Sölvell 2008, 7).

9. "CIs for clusters in areas designated by government as attractive perform significantly better in attracting new firms" (Ketels, Lindqvist, and Sölvell 2008, 7).

10. "For promoting cluster growth, establishing an exchange with other clusters in the same industry is beneficial" (Ketels, Lindqvist, and Sölvell 2008, 7).

11. "In developing and transition economies, there is usually less trust among companies and between companies and government than in advanced economies" (Ketels, Lindqvist, and Sölvell 2006, 6).

12. Advanced economies are all countries that fall outside the developing and transition classifications, or as Ketels, Lindqvist, and Sölvell (2006, 10) suggest: they are "high-income economies (OECD or non-OECD) which are not transition economies."

References

Chinitz, B. 1961. "Contrasts in Agglomeration: New York and Pittsburgh." *American Economic Review* 51: 279–89.

Cortright, J. 2006. "Making Sense of Clusters: Regional Competitiveness and Economic Development." Discussion paper, Metropolitan Policy Program, Brookings Institution. http://www.brookings.edu/~/media/Files/rc/reports/2006/03cities_cortright/20060313_Clusters.pdf.

Fujita, M., P. Krugman, and A. Venables. 1999. *The Spatial Economy: Cities, Regions and International Trade*. Cambridge, MA: MIT Press.

Glaeser, E. L., H. D. Kallal, J. A. Scheinkman, and A. Shleifer. 1992. "Growth in Cities." *Journal of Political Economy* 100: 1126–52.

Henderson, J. V. 1997. "Externalities and Industrial Development." *Journal of Urban Economics* 42: 449–79.

Hoover, E. M., and F. Giarratani. 1948. *The Location of Economic Activity*. New York: McGraw-Hill.

Isard, W. 1956. *Location and Space Economy*. Cambridge, MA: MIT Press.

Jacobs, J. 1969. *The Economy of Cities*. London: Penguin Books.

Ketels, C., G. Lindqvist, and Ö. Sölvell. 2006. "Cluster Initiatives in Developing and Transition Economies." Center for Strategy and Competitiveness, Stockholm School of Economics, Stockholm, Sweden.

———. 2008. "Clusters and Cluster Initiatives." Center for Strategy and Competitiveness, Stockholm School of Economics, Stockholm, Sweden. http://www.europe-innova.eu/c/document_library/get_file?folderId=148901&name=DLFE-9310.pdf.

Marshall, A. 1920. *Principles of Economics*. London: Macmillan.

Mills, K. G., E. B. Reynolds, and A. Reamer. 2008. "Clusters and Competitiveness: A New Federal Role for Stimulating Regional Economies." Metropolitan Policy Program, Brookings Institution, Washington, DC.

Nallari, R., B. Griffith, and S. Yusuf. 2012. *Geography of Growth: Spatial Economics and Competitiveness*. Washington, DC: World Bank.

Piore, M., and C. Sabel. 1984. *The Second Industrial Divide*. New York: Basic Books.

Porter, M. E. 1990. *The Competitive Advantage of Nations*. New York: Free Press.

———. 2001. "The Microeconomics of Development." Paper presented at the conference Competitiveness and Development: Vision and Priorities for Action, Caracas,

June 20–21. http://www.cid.harvard.edu/archive/andes/documents/presentations/caracas_0601/porter_competitivenessforum_062101.pdf.

———. 2008. "Clusters, Innovation, and Competitiveness: Findings and Implications for Policy." Paper prepared for European Presidency Conference on Innovation and Clusters, Stockholm, Sweden, January 23.

Porter, M. E., M. Delgado, C. Ketels, and S. Stern. 2008. "Moving to a New Global Competitiveness Index." In *The Global Competitiveness Report 2008–2009*, 43–63. Geneva: World Economic Forum; Stockholm, Sweden: Ivory Tower AB.

Rosenfeld, S. 1997. "Bringing Clusters into the Mainstream of Economic Development." *European Planning Studies* 5 (1): 3–23.

Sölvell, Ö., G. Lindqvist, and C. Ketels. 2003. *The Cluster Initiative Greenbook*. Stockholm, Sweden: Ivory Tower AB.

World Bank. 2009. *Clusters for Competitiveness: A Practical Guide and Policy Implications for Developing Cluster Initiatives*. Washington, DC: World Bank.

www.ingramcontent.com/pod-product-compliance
Lightning Source LLC
Chambersburg PA
CBHW081507200326
41518CB00015B/2406